Best-
Wild Plants of
Colorado
and the Rockies

Text and Photography by Cattail Bob Seebeck

WESTCLIFFE PUBLISHERS
www.westcliffepublishers.com

The author and publisher disclaim any liability for injury or loss that may result from following instructions in this book.

ISBN: 1-56579-275-0

Designers: Mark Mulvany & Tim George
Production Manager: Harlene Finn
Editor: Kiki Sayre
Published by: Westcliffe Publishers, Inc.
       P.O. Box 1261
       Englewood, Colorado 80150
       www.westcliffepublishers.com
Printed in: Hong Kong by H&Y LTD.

Publisher's Cataloging in Publication Data

Seebeck, Cattail Bob, 1954–
      Best-tasting wild plants of Colorado and the Rockies / text and
photography by Cattail Bob Seebeck.
          p. cm.
      Includes index.
      ISBN 1-56579-275-0
      1. Wild plants, Edible—Colorado—Identification.   2. Wild plants,
Edible—Rocky Mountains Region—Identification.   3. Wild plants,
Edible—Colorado—Pictorial works.   4. Wild plants, Edible—Rocky
Mountains Region—Pictorial works.   I. Title.
      QK98.5.U6S44   1998
      581.6'32'09788—dc21   97-43083
                                                     CIP

For more information about other fine books and calenders from Westcliffe Publishers, please contact your local bookstore, call us at 1-800-523-3692, write for our free color catalog, or visit us on the Web at www.westcliffepublishers.com.

Cover photos: Squaw paint, and (clockwise from top left:) violet, prickly pear, and asparagus.

Opposite page photo: Dorsey Lake, near Estes Park. A riparian habitat and one of Cattail Bob's numerous teaching sites.

Contents

Introduction

The need for a good field guide to wild edible plants in the Rocky Mountain area has been apparent to me since I began teaching back in 1975. To fill this need, I have provided six special features not found in other field guides:

1) **Four color photographs per plant** are furnished, showing pertinent features and seasonal growth changes. Various focal lengths—from close-up shots, to scenes of the whole plant, to perhaps a vista of the entire habitat—are employed.

2) Only the **best-tasting wild edibles** are included. Of course, personal tastes vary, so I have relied upon the taste testing done by the thousands of children attending my classes in public school systems throughout the Rockies. After all, children can't hide their honest reactions to new taste sensations.

3) **Plant information adjacent to the photographs** is provided so that readers don't have to flip through the guide to observe one or the other.

4) The focus is exclusively on the **southern and central Rocky Mountain region:** Colorado, Wyoming, Montana, New Mexico, Utah, and Idaho.

5) This work is separated into two sections: **low altitude (below 9,000 feet) and high altitude (above 9,000 feet).** Although some plants will be observed on both sides of this artificial boundary, they are listed in their respective sections according to availability at altitude.

6) This guide offers recipe suggestions for the budding wild gourmet to create his/her own **original recipes.**

This field guide also contains a section on poisonous plants with eight of the most important toxic plants of our region included. I recommend all wild plant foragers familiarize themselves with these plants, as some are lethal if ingested. (Also, see "Look-alikes" section for each plant.)

Caution: Carefully read the plant descriptions, and look closely at the photos in this guide. Plant identification must be accurate! Never eat any wild plant food if there is any doubt as to its positive identification. Remember, there are old foragers, and there are bold foragers, but there are no old, bold foragers!

Edible and poisonous mushrooms are difficult to identify, and are not included in this work.

Identification: As foragers face the challenge of wild plant identification, they will notice that, in general, it is easier in summer and autumn due to the many features that the plant develops (flowers, fruits, etc.). Conversely, the most difficult seasons for identification are winter and spring, due to lack of features.

Altitude and weather offer other possible identification challenges. The forager will find that plants enduring higher altitudes will generally be smaller than the same species found at lower altitudes. In addition, cooler and/or dryer summers will produce smaller plants, on average, than warmer and/or wetter summers.

Once positive identification is made, the wild food forager must still keep in mind possible adverse reactions to normally safe edible plants. Usually these reactions are minor and rarely, if ever, lethal. They may be due to either   made pollution on the plant or toxic compounds naturally absorbed by the plant. Problems may also arise from eating certain plants to excess—notably oxalic plants like lambs quarter, mountain sorrel, or even store-bought spinach! And the idiosyncracies of one's own digestive system can also be a factor. Therefore, it is always best to lightly sample any new food at first, taking note of any unusual symptoms. If there are none, then gradually increase your intake. Once again, caution is the watchword.

Now that the faint-hearted are frightened off. . .

We all want to learn about wild edible plants for various reasons. Perhaps we want to experience new flavors or learn new recipes. Maybe we seek to stretch our food budget, or add some healthful wild vegetables to those starchy, freeze-dried dinners while backpacking. Perhaps we are interested in outdoor survival, or the diet of ancient cultures. Whatever the motivation, they are all excellent reasons for learning wild edible plants.

Survival: Having been a wilderness survival instructor for many years, I would like to address the often incorrect information I see in the media regarding the need for finding and eating wild edible plants in survival situations.

First, there are voluntary and involuntary survival scenarios. Some people choose voluntarily to live off the land. This primitive lifestyle is challenging and fun. I wholeheartedly recommend learning the many skills our ancestors knew so well. Learning and using wild edible plants responsibly is an important aspect of this lifestyle.

However, true wilderness emergencies encountered by the average person in the Rockies are involuntary, and require different priorities. Most of these situations do not last long enough to warrant the need for finding wild plant food. In fact, searching for wild food may make a bad situation even worse (i.e. accidental poisoning, getting even more lost, expending valuable body energy unnecessarily, etc.).

In these "wait until rescue" wilderness survival events, finding wild plant food is a low priority. Higher priorities like maintaining normal body temperature, staying put, setting up shelter, signaling, firestarting, and staying dry (in a cold environment) and staying hydrated (in a hot environment), are all much more important than acquiring wild food. Hollywood survival films notwithstanding, we can survive for many days without food by conserving our energy, and rescue will probably occur before we starve to death—assuming someone noticed we were missing and crews are out looking for us.

There are many excellent survival schools located throughout the Rocky Mountain region. These institutions will help the student understand the finer points of establishing priorities for varying survival scenarios.

Harvesting: Certain methods of harvesting affect plants more than others. Acce͏͏   the entire root system, for example, will most certainly kill the plant, whereas simply plucking a few fruits or berries will be beneficial, as it spreads the seeds. Harvest for sustainability. Small quantities should be sufficient for most purposes, but always practice the harvesting ethic when collecting wild edible roots and/or other plant parts. Harvest no more than 25 percent of a plant community, and leave the remainder untouched to produce seed for the next growing season. Seeds should also be sown to replace what has been taken. Do not overharvest and do not harvest solitary plants.

Environmental responsibility is not just today's catchphrase. It is a lifestyle we all must embrace if the human species is to continue to flourish as a contributor to the great wheel of life on our planet. Think about your harvesting, and aim for perpetuation of the wild plant community.

Wild plants that you plan on using frequently should be grown yourself at home, or purchased from a commercial source. Many wild plants are easily grown from seed collected in August and September.

Wild plants may also be purchased from local greenhouses ready for planting. Wild plants or their seed should be planted in locations that are identical to the wild microhabitat that they are normally found growing in. If you duplicate the soil type, moisture content, and lighting conditions, you should have success in growing and harvesting your favorite wild edible plants.

Check with local authorities before harvesting on public land, and always get permission before harvesting on private land. Do not harvest from heavily traveled roadsides, or sprayed or polluted areas.

Once harvesting is complete, try to use the plants quickly, if possible, while they are still fresh. Cutting edible flowers and greens a few inches down the stem, then spraying with water or transporting plant material in cold water, will help prevent premature wilting.

Preparation: Now the preparation process begins. Rinse all plants well with potable water, especially aquatic plants, and plants to be used fresh. (Giardia micro-organisms may be present on aquatic plants.) Use flowers or other delicate plant parts quickly before they dry out. Cooked greens are often best when cooked lightly. Try to use as many colors and textures as possible for a finer presentation. Kitchen utensils such as blenders, processors, and flour mills greatly expand our wild foods repertoire, while dehydrating, canning, pickling, and freezing allow us to enjoy the fruits of our labor well into the winter. Recipe suggestions are offered in the "Use" category for each wild edible plant featured in this guide.

Nutrition: The nutritional analysis of wild plant foods is still in its infancy today. Yet, it is reasonable to assume that, overall, wild vegetables are just as nutritious as cultivated vegetables—perhaps even more so. Vegetables, however, do not provide much protein unless they are combined properly. To real diet sufficient in quality protein sans meat, a serving must be eaten these three food categories within about 48 hours: 1) grains, 2) seeds, and 3) beans (or nuts). The protein synthesis occurs in the bloodstream, not in the digestive tract, as many people falsely believe. Thus, a grain food may be eaten one day, beans the next, and a high-quality, complete protein diet is still achieved. Unfortunately, we do not have many wild edible beans in our region; however, the Rocky Mountains are abundant in wild edible grains and seeds.

Most of us are not strict vegetarians, and our probable treatment of edible wild plants will be to augment our garden-grown or store-bought staples. However, armed with the information in this guide, the student can also create unique gourmet meals that will stimulate both conversation, as well as appetite! These meals will take you back to a simpler time—a time when people lived closer to nature and fine dining was a rare special event.

Gourmet meals: To give the reader an idea of the possibilities, the following is an example of a meal embellished in "wild" gourmet style. The setting should be outdoors, weather permitting. Otherwise, anywhere quiet, natural, and elegant will do.

To begin the meal, serve a wild grape wine apéritif, with a wildflower salad, seasoned lightly using a hazelnut oil vinegrette. Complement with wild nettle-onion soup, warm amaranth rolls, and wild herb butter.

The main entree of pan-fried trout may be garnished with chopped sorrel leaf, gooseberry, or juniper. A sidedish of steamed watercress and milkweed lightly seasoned with wild mustard seed and wild parsley, accompany this entree nicely. Perhaps a dessert of homemade wild peppermint chip ice cream will bring everyone gently back to reality.

I expect your guests will be quite impressed, and with the application of this field guide, many more similar meals await the student's own special touch!

In conclusion: By 1900, much of the ancient wild plant knowledge of this continent had been lost, along with the immoral destruction of the native cultures that knew the flora so well. Now, it is up to us, the new stewards of this land, to relearn the wise use of these plants, imparting our own cultural style and personality. The "wild-forager-gourmet-chef" has great latitude for experimentation, ultimately shaping a heretofore, completely unknown wild food neo-cuisine. With imagination and a little common-sense cookery, we can create a mealtime ambience of profound beauty and unparalleled taste that fosters a deep kinship with nature, and with those noble men, women, and children who once walked where we walk today. May this work help preserve and expand their knowledge
e generations. Bon appetit!

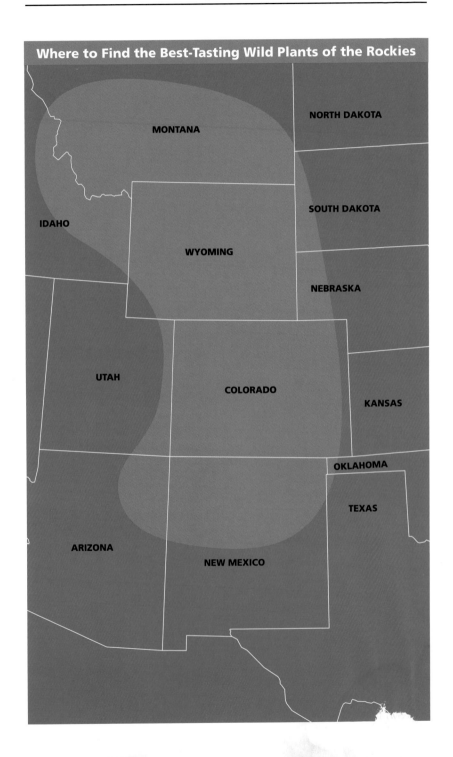

Using This Guide

COMMON NAME (in alphabetical order); ***Botanical nomenclature.***

Other names: Listed here are other common names in use.

Altitude: These are the altitudinal limits of habitat for this plant. All altitudinal measurements are in feet above sea level.

Description: Here, find a not-too-technical botanical description.

Macrohabitat: This is the overall kind of locality in which a plant grows, often covering entire states or mountain ranges.

Microhabitat: The immediate, local, surrounding community in which a plant grows, including light and soil conditions, is listed here.

Plant growth phases: This table correlates plant growth phases to altitude and months in the growing season (April–Oct.). For the purposes of this table, low altitude is considered below 6,500 feet. Middle altitude is between 6,500 and 9,000 feet. And high altitude is considered above 9,000 feet.

Best-tasting parts: Self-explanatory.

Use: This section gives the forager ideas for creating meals with the particular plant featured. Simply substitute the wild edible plants with similar vegetables in your favorite recipes. Be creative!

Look-alikes: When immature–this is a listing of flora that look like the featured plant before flowering.
When mature–a listing of "look-alikes" after flowering. Almost all plants are easier to identify during or after flowering.
All toxic look-alikes are labeled as such.

Note: Here, find miscellaneous information about the featured plant.

AMARANTH (Amaranthus hybridus, A. powelii, A. retroflexus)

Other names: Pigweed, redroot, alegría, careless weed.

Altitude: 4,000–8,500 feet.

Description: Annual. Herbaceous. Weedy. Height to 6 feet. The root, and sometimes the stem, are reddish-colored. Leaves are·oval and 1 to 3-inches long. Flowers are green and inconspicuous. When the green flower spikes dry out and turn brown, the tiny, shiny black seeds are ready to harvest. Amaranth can be found growing in groups or solitary. As an annual, it will only live for one season.

Macrohabitat: Common throughout our region below 7,000 feet.

Microhabitat: Disturbed soil; around human habitation. Damp-to-dry soil.

Plant Growth Phases		
Lower Altitudes	**Middle Altitudes**	**Higher Altitudes**
APRIL Sprouting	Dormant	Rare
MAY Leaf/stem growth	Sprouting	"
JUNE Leaf/stem growth	Leaf/stem growth	"
JULY Flowering	Flowering	"
AUG. Mature seeds	Immature seeds	"
SEPT. Mature seeds	Mature seeds	"
OCT. Seeds are harvestable through the winter		"

Best-tasting parts: Leaves, seeds.

Use: Raw or cooked. Mild flavor. Fresh leaves are good in salads, tacos, rice dishes, and on sandwiches. Cooked in omelets, lasagne, soups, and egg rolls. Roasted lightly, seeds may be ground into flour or boiled as a hot cereal. Seeds may also be popped like popcorn, or sprouted. Harvest seed and chaff with gloves (the chaff is somewhat spiny), and winnow chaff from the seed using the wind.

Look-alikes: When immature–many.
             When mature–poison suckleya (mildly toxic, not common); lambs quarter (edible; see lambs quarter); saltbrush (edible; see saltbrush).

Note: This is a very nutritious seed, high in essential amino acid or protein content.

APPLE *(Malus spp.)*

Other names: Wild apple.

Altitude: 4,000–8,500 feet.

Description: Perennial. Arborescent. Deciduous. Height to 40 feet. Smooth bark is reddish, bronze, or gray. Leaves are oval-shaped with tiny teeth around the leaf edges. Showy pink or white flowers are 1½ to 2-inches wide, and in clusters. Fruits are the same as store-bought, perhaps a bit smaller on average. Apple trees are usually found growing solitary. Autumn leaf colors are yellow. These trees produce the largest wild fruit and the most abundant single-source crop in the Rockies.

Macrohabitat: Scattered throughout the Rocky Mountain region; mostly found under 7,000 feet.

Microhabitat: Near human habitation: trailsides, campsites, canyon bottoms and roadsides. Damp-to-dry soil.

Plant Growth Phases		
Lower Altitudes	**Middle Altitudes**	**Higher Altitudes**
APRIL Flowering	Dormant	Rare
MAY Flowering	Flowering	"
JUNE Immature fruits	Immature fruits	"
JULY Immature fruits	Immature fruits	"
AUG. Unripe/ripe fruits	Unripe/ripe fruits	"
SEPT. Ripe fruits	Ripe fruits	"
OCT. Most fruit fallen	Most fruit fallen	"

Best-tasting parts: Fruits (apples).

Use: Usually sour flavor. Use just like store-bought apples—in pies, turnovers, fruit leather, glaze, jelly, wine, vinegar, smoothies, and homemade ice cream. May be sliced and dehydrated.

Look-alikes: When immature–chokecherry, plum, serviceberry, pin cherry (all edible fruits).

When mature–none.

Caution: Like the seeds of most commercial fruit, apple seeds are poisonous.

Note: Johnny Appleseed notwithstanding, our many varieties of wild apple trees today are the result of people tossing their apple cores along trailsides and roadsides. Also, it is rare to find wild crabapple growing in the Rockies.

ASPARAGUS *(Asparagus officinalis)*

Other names: Common asparagus, golden asparagus.

Altitude: 4,000–8,500 feet.

Description: Perennial. Herbaceous. Ornamental. A bushy, feathery-looking shrub when mature. Height to 7 feet. Leafy branches have a somewhat pine needle-type look. Individual leaflets are linear and very small. Tiny, yellow (sometimes white) bell-shaped flowers are ¼-inch long. Green berries, ¼ inch in diameter, turn red. (The berries are not edible.) Asparagus is usually found growing in solitary clumps, several-to-many stems per clump. Autumn colors are yellow. It dies back to ground level each winter. Learning to identify the dried, tan, dead shrub in the spring yields the young, tender shoots found beneath it.

Macrohabitat: Throughout our region; common below 6,000 feet.

Microhabitat: River bottomland, meadows, and fencerows. Damp soil.

Plant Growth Phases		
	Lower Altitudes	**Middle Altitudes**	**Higher Altitudes**
APRIL	Sprouting (shoots)	Dormant	Rare
MAY	Sprouting (shoots)	Sprouting (shoots)	"
JUNE	Branching/flowering	Sprouting/branching	"
JULY	Flowering/berries	Flowering	"
AUG.	Red berries (toxic)	Green/red berries	"
SEPT.	Red berries (toxic)	Red berries (toxic)	"
OCT.	Bush turns yellow, then light tan through winter		"

Best-tasting parts: Young shoots (after branching, they become too tough and fibrous to eat).

Use: Use just like store-bought asparagus. Try fresh or lightly steamed. Also good in casseroles, omelets, rice pilaf, crepes, and soup.

Look-alikes: When immature–none.
                    When mature–none.

Note: Wild asparagus is becoming more difficult to find in populated areas due to overharvesting. As with any wild plant you plan to use often, I recommend growing your own.

BEEPLANT *(Cleome serrulata, C. lutea)*

Other names: Spider plant, Rocky Mountain beeplant.

Altitude: 4,000–8,500 feet.

Description: Annual. Herbaceous. Erect. Ornamental. Leaves exhibit a triple leaflet arrangement. Leaflets are 1 to 4-inches long. Showy flowers are usually pink on the east side of the Continental Divide, and both yellow and pink west of the divide. Fruit is a green bean-like pod, 1 to 3-inches long, below the flowers. Beeplant is found growing in dispersed groupings or sometimes solitary. As an annual, it lives only one season.

Macrohabitat: Scattered throughout our region.

Microhabitat: Sunny, open meadows. Damp-to-dry soil.

Plant Growth Phases		
Lower Altitudes	**Middle Altitudes**	**Higher Altitudes**
APRIL Dormant	Dormant	Rare
MAY Sprouting	Dormant/sprouting	"
JUNE Leaf/stalk growth	Leaf growth	"
JULY Flower buds	Leaf/stalk growth	"
AUG. Flowering/seedpods	Flowering	"
SEPT. Seedpods	Flowering/seedpods	"
OCT. Dried seedpods	Dried seedpods	"

Best-tasting parts: Young seedpods.

Use: Pods are hot and spicy when fresh. Cooking or drying reduces spiciness. Great fresh in salads, homemade salad dressing, salsa, pesto, chip dip, tacos, or lightly cooked in stir-fries. Young sprouts are also edible, but difficult to identify.

Look-alikes: When immature–many (some toxic).
    When mature–sweet pea (see Toxic Plants).

Caution: Most wild bean pods in the Rockies are moderately poisonous. Do not eat beeplant unless identification is positive.

Note: I have grown beeplant easily from seed on my property at 7,000 feet. It is related to the garden ornamental spiderplant.

BLACK MUSTARD *(Brassica nigra)*

Other names: Wild mustard.

Altitude: 4,000–8,000 feet.

Description: Annual. Herbaceous. Height to 8 feet. This is the tallest wild mustard in our region. Large lower leaves; smaller and less numerous on the upper stem when mature. Has a showy raceme of yellow, four-petaled flowers and linear seedpods in typical mustard "squirrel-tail" form (see Glossary). Usually grows with others in the neighborhood; sometimes solitary. As an annual, black mustard only lives one season.

Macrohabitat: Throughout our region, mostly under 5,500 feet. Not common.

Microhabitat: Rich, moist soil; river bottomland; disturbed soil.

Plant Growth Phases		
Lower Altitudes	**Middle Altitudes**	**Higher Altitudes**
APRIL Dormant	Dormant	Rare
MAY Sprouting	Dormant/Sprouting	"
JUNE Leaf growth	Leaf growth	"
JULY Stalk growth	Leaf/stalk growth	"
AUG. Flowering	Flowering	"
SEPT. Flowers/seedpods	Flowers/seedpods	"
OCT. Frost damage	Frost damage	"

Best-tasting parts: Leaves and seeds.

Use: Very hot, spicy, horseradish flavor. Great raw in salads, salsa, ranch omelets, and on sandwiches. Cooking and drying reduce spiciness. Seeds can be sprouted or ground into a paste, mixed with a little salt, vinegar, and toasted flour to thicken, making a table mustard condiment.

Look-alikes: When immature–many.
When mature–other mustard family members.

Caution: Wild mustards have been known to cause intestinal irritation when eaten to excess.

Note: This plant is used to make a commercial table mustard condiment. Most wild mustards can be easily propagated from seed.

CAMOMILE *(Matricaria matricarioides var. suaveolens, M. discoidea)*

Other names: Wild camomile, pineapple weed, May weed, false camomile, Manzinilla del Barrio.

Altitude: 4,000–10,500 feet.

Description: Annual. Herbaceous. Aromatic. Height to 12 inches. A small plant, difficult to see from a distance. Easiest to find when in flower. Delicate, many-dissected leaves. Yellow-green terminal flowerheads—without flower petals—smell somewhat like pineapple. It is found growing in dispersed groups or colonies; rarely solitary. Camomile dies back to ground level each winter.

Macrohabitat: Common throughout our region, below 9,000 feet.

Microhabitat: Trailsides, dirt roads, parking lots. Sandy, well-drained soil. Often found growing beneath the existing vegetation.

Plant Growth Phases		
Lower Altitudes	**Middle Altitudes**	**Higher Altitudes**
APRIL Sprouting	Dormant	Dormant
MAY Leaf growth	Sprouting	Dormant
JUNE Some flowering	Leaf growth	Sprouting
JULY Flowering/seeds	Some flowering	Leaf growth
AUG. Dries up	Flowering/seeds	Flowering/seeds
SEPT. Dried, brown stalk	Dries up	Dries up
OCT. Hard to find	Hard to find	Hard to find

Best-tasting parts: Flowers, leaves.

Use: Dried for tea, or flowers fresh in salads. Only flowers have the pineapple flavor. Camomile is easily propagated from the tiny seeds.

Look-alikes: When immature–poison hemlock (poisonous; much larger when mature; see Toxic Plants), tansy mustard (edible).
When mature–blister buttercup (toxic; similar flower, but it grows in wet soil and has a very different leaf).

Note: Wild camomile tea acts as a mild sedative, especially for children.

CATTAIL *(Typha latifolia, T. angustifolia)*

Other names: Cat o' nine tails, common cattail, cattail flag.

Altitude: 4,000–9,000 feet.

Description: Perennial. Herbaceous. Marsh or aquatic plants. Height to 7 feet. Creeping rootstocks. Large, flat, grass-like leaves. Sausage-shaped flower/fruit, 6–18-inches tall, ½ to 1¼ inches in diameter. Cattail grows in colonies, almost never solitary. It dies back to ground level each winter.

Macrohabitat: Abundant at lowest altitudes; less common in higher altitudes.

Microhabitat: Wet places. Bogs. Marshes. In or near water sources.

Plant Growth Phases			
	Lower Altitudes	**Middle Altitudes**	**Higher Altitudes**
APRIL	Sprouting (shoots)	Dormant	Rare
MAY	Leaf growth	Sprouting (shoots)	"
JUNE	Green fruit/pollen	Leaf growth	"
JULY	Fruit dries out	Green fruit/pollen	"
AUG.	Downy seedhead	Fruit dries out	"
SEPT.	Downy seedhead	Downy seedhead	"
OCT.	Root available through winter if soil is not too frozen for digging		

Best-tasting parts: Shoots, roots, inner core, fruit, pollen.

Use: Access roots with a digging tool. Clean the roots and pound/shred in a tub of water. Suspended starch will settle overnight. Pour top water off. Dry out this material, then grind into flour. Has a high starch content. Before mid-summer, peel away all outer leaves to access tender inner core. Use raw or cooked. Tastes like cucumber. Immature, green seed-spike (sausage-shaped fruit) is edible cooked. Prepare and eat like corn on the cob; great flavor! Yellow pollen above green seed-spike can be collected by bending the spike and shaking it into a sack. Use like flour. Shoots are also edible. The leaves can be woven for baskets, mats, etc. The dry, downy seeds may be used for fire-starting tinder.

Look-alikes: When immature–iris (toxic; leaves are smaller; roots are similar to cattail).
      When mature–none.

Note: Cattail should only be harvested in abundant stands found at lower altitudes. It is infrequent-to-rare in the high country.

CHICORY *(Cichorium intybus)*

Other names: Succory.

Altitude: 4,000–7,500 feet.

Description: Perennial. Herbaceous. Height to 5 feet. Basal leaves first, then branching upper flowering stems almost devoid of leaves. Showy blue flowers, 1-inch in diameter, are borne in axils of leaves. Fruit is capsule-like. Dark seeds. Chicory is found growing in colonies or solitary. It dies back to ground level each winter.

Macrohabitat: Abundant in some areas, uncommon in others.

Microhabitat: Sunny meadows, fencerows, road sides. Damp soil.

Plant Growth Phases			
	Lower Altitudes	**Middle Altitudes**	**Higher Altitudes**
APRIL	Sprouting	Dormant	Rare
MAY	Leaf growth	Sprouting	"
JUNE	Stalk begins	Stalk begins	"
JULY	Flower buds	Flower buds	"
AUG.	Flowering	Flowering	"
SEPT.	Flowering/seeds	Flowering/seeds	"
OCT.	Recognizing dried seedstalk in winter yields edible root		

Best-tasting parts: Roots.

Use: Roots make a good coffee-like beverage after processing. First clean, then cut or saw roots into small pieces. Roast pieces in an oven at 350 degrees for about one hour, then grind root pieces up into a coffee ground-like texture. Use this as you would coffee. Many commercial coffees are cut with Chicory root. Seeds can also be sprouted.

Look-alikes: When immature–dandelion (can be used similarly).
When mature–none.

Note: I have grown chicory easily from seed around my home at 7,000 feet. Each season there are more, as it reseeds itself. The blue flowers are quite striking.

CHOKECHERRY *(Prunus virginiana var. melanocarpa)*

Other names: Black chokecherry, chokeberry, capulín.

Altitude: 4,000–9,000 feet.

Description: Perennial. Arborescent. Deciduous. Small tree. Height to 25 feet. Smooth, dark-gray bark (reddish at the tips). Pointed, oval leaves with tiny teeth around edges. Showy, aromatic raceme of whitish-yellow flowers. The immature fruits are first green, then red, then black. Each cherry contains a single pit or seed. Chokecherry is found growing in thickets or solitary. Autumn leaf color is typically reddish. Of all the wild fruits in our region, the Chokecherry species, as a whole, produce the greatest fruit quantities.

Macrohabitat: Very common throughout our region. Most fruit production occurs below 8,000 feet.

Microhabitat: Sunny meadows, creekbanks, damp valley bottoms.

Plant Growth Phases		
	Lower Altitudes	**Middle Altitudes**	**Higher Altitudes**
APRIL	Leaves emerge	Leaves emerge	Rare
MAY	Flowering	Leaves	"
JUNE	Immature cherries	Flowering	"
JULY	Green cherries	Immature cherries	"
AUG.	Ripe, black cherries	Red/black cherries	"
SEPT.	Ripe, black cherries	Ripe, black cherries	"
OCT.	Dried cherries may be found on branches until mid-winter		

Best-tasting parts: Fruits (cherries).

Use: Only the black cherries are edible. All other parts of this plant are mildly poisonous—even the unripe red cherries. Ripe cherries can provide jelly, syrup, gelatin, wine, juice, fruit leather, and pemmican. Screen out the seeds. Dehydration preserves cherries for very long periods.

Look-alikes: When immature–plum (edible fruit), pin cherry (edible fruit). When mature–pin cherry (edible fruit).

Note: Like many commercial fruits, the seeds of chokecherry are mildly poisonous. Drying and heat evaporate toxic principles.

COTA *(Thelesperma megapotamicum var. gracile)*

Other names: Greenthread, Navaho tea, Indian tea.

Altitude: 4,000–8,000 feet.

Description: Perennial. Erect. Wiry-looking when mature. Height to 2 feet. Very few upper leaves. Many threadlike basal leaves. Usually gray-green leaf and stem color. Flowers are golden. Cota is mostly found in large groupings; rarely solitary. It dies back to ground level each winter.

Macrohabitat: Most common in the southern Rocky Mountains, below 6,000 feet.

Microhabitat: Open meadows. Somewhat dry soil.

Plant Growth Phases		
Lower Altitudes	**Middle Altitudes**	**Higher Altitudes**
APRIL Leaves emerge	Dormant	Rare
MAY Flower stalk begins	Leaves emerge	"
JUNE Flower buds	Flower stalk begins	"
JULY Flowering	Flower buds	"
AUG. Flowering, drying	Flowering	"
SEPT. Few flowers, drying	Few flowers, drying	"
OCT. Brown, dry stems and seedheads		"

Best-tasting parts: Dried flowers, stems, and leaves.

Use: A good tasting tea, prepared by Native Americans for thousands of years.

Look-alikes: When immature–many (some toxic).
When mature–none.

Note: Cota is more common in our southern regions. In the northern regions, where it is not as common, Cota should not be over-harvested. Grow it yourself if you plan to use it frequently.

EVENING PRIMROSE *(Oenothera strigosa var. biennis, O. hookeri)*

Other names: Sundrops.

Altitude: 4,000–10,000 feet.

Description: Biennial. Herbaceous. Sometimes evergreen. Taproot. Round rosette of leaves the first year, flowering stalk the second year; height to 5 feet. Four-petaled, 1-inch wide bright yellow flowers, on the upper stem. Each leaf has a light green midrib and the main stem is reddish. Reddish-purple rosettes last through winter. Usually solitary growth. Evening primrose dies after the second year.

Macrohabitat: Common throughout our region below 8,000 feet.

Microhabitat: Open, sunny meadows; disturbed soil. Dry or damp.

Plant Growth Phases *(Second year growth)*			
	Lower Altitudes	**Middle Altitudes**	**Higher Altitudes**
APRIL	Rosettes	Rosettes	Dormant
MAY	Stalk begins	Rosettes	Rosettes
JUNE	Stalk, flower buds	Stalk begins	Rosettes
JULY	Flowering	Flowering	Stalk begins
AUG.	Flowering/seedpods	Flowering/seedpods	Flowering
SEPT.	Flowering/seedpods	Flowering/seedpods	Flowering/seedpods
OCT.	Identifying first-year rosettes in winter yields edible root		

Best-tasting parts: Roots, leaves, flowers, flower buds.

Use: Mild flavor. Raw or cooked. Roots are tender before the flower stalk appears, tough afterwards (second year). Slice in salads, casseroles, omelets, soups, and stir-fries. Use leaves and flowers in salads, marinades, rice dishes, lasagne, nut loaf, and meat loaf. Young seedpods are also edible. Seeds may be roasted and ground into flour.

Look-alikes: When immature–(first year) many.
When mature–(second year) none.

Note: Less common stemless evening primroses are also edible. Do not confuse the evening primrose family (edible) with the primrose family (not edible). The names are similar, but they are very different plant families.

GOLDEN CURRANT *(Ribes aureum var. longiflorum, R. odoratum)*

Other names: Buffalo currant, clove bush, clove currant.

Altitude: 4,000–8,000 feet.

Description: Perennial. Deciduous. Woody shrub. Usually spineless. Height to 6 feet. Yellow, tubular-shaped flowers are sometimes aromatic. Leaves are more deeply cleft than other currants. The berry is smooth, usually shiny black, sometimes red/orange, and translucent. The conspicuous dried flower stays attached to the fruit (like most currants). Seeds are soft. Autumn leaf colors are red. Grows as a solitary shrub.

Macrohabitat: Throughout our region. Most common below 6,000 feet.

Microhabitat: Sunny hillsides, valley floors. Damp soil.

Plant Growth Phases		
Lower Altitudes	**Middle Altitudes**	**Higher Altitudes**
APRIL Leaves/flowering	Leaves emerge	Rare
MAY Flowering	Flowering	"
JUNE Immature berries	Immature berries	"
JULY Unripe berries	Unripe berries	"
AUG. Ripe berries	Unripe/ripe berries	"
SEPT. Ripe berries	Ripe berries	"
OCT. A few dried berries are found on the bush through winter		

Best-tasting parts: Berries (currants).

Use: Berries make good jam, syrup, fruit leather, pemmican, wine, gelatin, and juice. Dehydrated berries last many years. Flowers are also edible.

Look-alikes: When immature–other currant family members.
When mature–other currant family members.

Note: All currants (except some of the hi-bush currants) display the persistent, conspicuous dried spindle on the fruit. This is the remnant of the earlier spring flower (see photo). This feature makes currant easy to identify.

GOOSEBERRY *(Ribes inerme var. saxosum)*

Other names: Black currant.

Altitude: 5,000–11,000 feet.

Description: Perennial. Deciduous. Woody shrub. Height to 5 feet. Width to 5 feet. Almost always spiny. Stems often gracefully arch out from the center when not crowded by other flora. Leaves are roundish in outline and lobed. Flowers are greenish-white/pink. The conspicuous dried flower stays attached to the fruit (like most currants). The berry is smooth and somewhat translucent purple. Seeds are small and soft. Grows as a solitary shrub. Autumn leaf colors are yellow or red.

Macrohabitat: Common throughout our region in foothills and mountains. Mostly found between 5,000 and 9,000 feet.

Microhabitat: Canyon bottoms, creek banks, meadows. Damp soil.

Plant Growth Phases		
Lower Altitudes	**Middle Altitudes**	**Higher Altitudes**
APRIL Leaves emerge	Dormant	Dormant
MAY Flowering	Leaves/flowering	Dormant
JUNE Immature berries	Flowering	Leaves/flowering
JULY Unripe berries	Immature berries	Flowering
AUG. Ripe berries	Unripe/ripe berries	Unripe berries
SEPT. Ripe berries	Ripe berries	Ripe berries
OCT. Few dried berries remain on the shrub through the winter		

Best-tasting parts: Berries (currants).

Use: Very tart, sour flavor. Excellent fresh in cold or hot cereal. Gooseberry is also used to make jam, syrup, fruit leather, wine, pemmican, and gelatin. It can be juiced. Good mixed with other fruits as well.

Look-alikes: When immature–other currant family members.
When mature–other currant family members.

Note: Our gooseberry is not the commercial, midwestern, green gooseberry sold in stores. All currants (except some of the hi-bush currants) display the persistent, conspicuous dried spindle on the fruit. This is the remnant of the earlier spring flower (see photo). This feature makes currant easy to identify.

GRAPE *(Vitis vulpina, V. arizonica)*

Other names: Wild grapevine, frost grape.

Altitude: 4,000–7,000 feet.

Description: Perennial. Deciduous. Woody vines. Climbing by tendrils to 20 feet or more. Leaves grow to 6 inches in diameter. Young stems are reddish. The flowers are inconspicuous in pyramidal clusters. Fruits are green, then bluish-purple, with a bloom, giving it a frosted look. Seeds are small and hard. Grape will be found growing either solitary or in small groupings.

Macrohabitat: Most common in the southern and eastern Rockies. Found mostly below 6,500 feet.

Microhabitat: Canyon floors, creek banks, forested, shaded areas. Damp soil.

Plant Growth Phases		
Lower Altitudes	**Middle Altitudes**	**Higher Altitudes**
APRIL Leaf buds open	Dormant	Rare
MAY Pyramidal flowers	Leaf buds	"
JUNE Immature grapes	Pyramidal flowers	"
JULY Unripe grapes	Immature grapes	"
AUG. Ripe grapes	Unripe grapes	"
SEPT. Ripe grapes	Ripe grapes	"
OCT. Frost-damaged leaves; some dried fruits available on the vine until about Dec.		

Best-tasting parts: Leaves, tendrils, and fruit (grapes).

Use: Leaves are mildly flavored. Tendrils are sour, but dry out quickly and lose sourness. Grapes are tart. They make good jelly, syrup, juice, gelatin, and wine. (Screen out the seeds.) Leaves are used to wrap traditional Middle Eastern foods. Tendrils are great raw in salads.

Look-alikes: When immature–squashberry (edible fruit), hops vine, mock cucumber vine, clematis vine.

When mature–Virginia creeper (toxic vine, similar fruit, very different leaves).

Note: Grapevine may be grown from nursery stock anywhere in our area below 7,500 feet.

HAZELNUT *(Corylus cornuta)*

Other names: Filbert, beaked hazelnut.

Altitude: 5,000–8,000 feet.

Description: Perennial. Arborescent. Deciduous. Small tree or woody shrub. Height to 6 feet. Toothed leaves are 2 to 5-inches long. Flowers are inconspicuous. The edible nut, ½ inch in diameter, is encased in a hard shell which is inside a fuzzy, beaked husk about 2-inches long. The nuts are often found growing in pairs. Hazelnut often grows as a thicket. It is not a plentiful nut producer in our region. Autumn leaf colors are yellow.

Macrohabitat: Rare in our southwestern regions; scattered elsewhere. Mostly below 7,000 feet.

Microhabitat: Forested terrain; along creeks.

Plant Growth Phases			
	Lower Altitudes	**Middle Altitudes**	**Higher Altitudes**
APRIL	Leaves emerge	Dormant	Rare
MAY	Inconspicuous flowers	Leaves emerge	"
JUNE	Immature nuts	Inconspicuous flowers	"
JULY	Unripe nuts	Immature nuts	"
AUG.	Ripe nuts	Unripe/ripe nuts	"
SEPT.	Ripe nuts	Ripe nuts	"
OCT.	Few nuts left	Few nuts left	

Best-tasting parts: Nuts.

Use: Excellent flavor. Use in any recipe requiring nuts. Hazelnut butter and roasted/salted hazelnuts are great!

Look-alikes: When immature–river alders and birches.
When mature–river alders and birches.

Note: Alders and birches have a small (about 1-inch long) pendant, fruiting structure that looks somewhat like a tiny pine cone, and their bark is darker, sometimes shiny, almost purplish in color.

HOLLY GRAPE *(Berberis repens)*

Other names: Oregon grape, creeping barberry, creeping mahonia.

Altitude: 5,000–10,000 feet.

Description: Perennial. Evergreen. Xerophytic. Ornamental. Height to 18 inches. Low growth habit. Woody stem; a yellow wood color. Clusters of yellow flowers. Compound leaves; leaflets 1 to 2-inches long, with a few spines along the leaf edges. Pale underneath leaflets. Fruit is dark blue when ripe, ½ inch in diameter, and covered with a whitish bloom giving it a frosted look. Seeds are small and soft. Holly grape is found growing in dispersed colonies or solitary. Winter leaf colors are reddish-purple. Usually some reddish leaf color is found year-round. Fruit production is erratic in our region. Like most fruits, some years are better than others.

Macrohabitat: In mountainous topography throughout our region. Best fruit production is usually below 8,000 feet.

Microhabitat: Pine forests, especially ponderosa. Dry, sunny slopes.

Plant Growth Phases		
Lower Altitudes	**Middle Altitudes**	**Higher Altitudes**
APRIL Flowering	Dormant	Dormant
MAY Flowering	Flowering	Dormant
JUNE Green fruits	Flowering	Flowering
JULY Unripe/ripe fruits	Green fruits	Flowering
AUG. Ripe fruits	Ripe fruits	Green fruits
SEPT. Ripe fruits	Ripe fruits	Ripe fruits
OCT. A few dried fruits are found on the plants through the winter		

Best-tasting parts: Fruits.

Use: Strong, sour flavor. Fruits make good jelly, syrup, wine, lemonade, gelatin, sauce, and fruit leather. Combine with other fruits if flavor is too strong.

Look-alikes: When immature–other barberry family members.
When mature–other barberry family members.

Note: The other barberry species appear similar, however, they usually display a larger, shrubby-growth habit, and are found in our southwestern regions. They offer edible fruit as well.

HORSEMINT *(Monarda fistulosa, M. menthaefolia)*

Other names: Bee balm, wild oregano, Oswego tea, fire and ice, bergamot, orégano de la Sierra.

Altitude: 4,000–9,000 feet.

Description: Perennial. Herbaceous. Aromatic. Purplish-colored sprouts. Height to 2 feet when mature. Flowers are showy, terminal, pinkish (rarely white), 1 to 3 inches in diameter, eventually becoming globular seedheads. The stem is square. Opposite leaves to 3-inches long, with light green midribs. Horsemint is found growing in colonies; rarely solitary. It dies back to ground level each winter.

Macrohabitat: Throughout our region. Most common from foothills to about 8,500 feet.

Microhabitat: Sunny fields, meadows, canyon bottoms. Damp soil.

Plant Growth Phases		
Lower Altitudes	**Middle Altitudes**	**Higher Altitudes**
APRIL Sprouting	Sprouting	Rare
MAY Stem, leaf growth	Stem, leaf growth	"
JUNE Flower buds	Flower buds	"
JULY Flowering	Flowering	"
AUG. Flowering	Flowering	"
SEPT. Seedheads	Seedheads	"
OCT. Dried stems and seedheads help identify horsemint in dormant months		

Best-tasting parts: Leaves, flower buds, flowers.

Use: Spicy-hot flavor when fresh, especially flowers. Excellent in salsa, chili, pasta sauce, and pesto. An oregano spice substitute, tea, and garnish. Seeds may be sprouted. Leaves may be dried. Drying or cooking reduces hot spiciness, but not flavor.

Look-alikes: When immature–many.
When mature–other mint family members.

Note: If it is found wild in our region, has a square stem, and is mint-scented, it is safe to eat. Also, horsemint can be easily propagated from seed in damp bottomland, and young leaves can be harvested as early as March.

LAMBS QUARTER *(Chenopodium berlandieri, C. album, C. fremontii)*

Other names: Goosefoot, wild spinach, pigweed.

Altitude: 4,000–9,500 feet.

Description: Annual. Herbaceous. Weedy. Height to 8 feet. Typical height is 1 to 3 feet. Leaves are goosefoot-shaped or more narrow, 2 to 5-inches long, with a lighter coloration on new growth at the tip, and often have red stripes on the stem. The inconspicuous flowers are in green clumps. Produces many small, dark seeds. Lambs quarter is found growing either solitary or in colonies. It dies back to ground level each winter.

Macrohabitat: Common. Town and country.

Microhabitat: Rich soil. Disturbed soil. Damp to dry.

Plant Growth Phases		
Lower Altitudes	**Middle Altitudes**	**Higher Altitudes**
APRIL Sprouting	Dormant	Rare
MAY Stem, leaf growth	Sprouting	"
JUNE Flower clusters	Stem, leaf growth	"
JULY Flower clusters	Flower clusters	"
AUG. Leaves and seeds	Leaves and seeds	"
SEPT. Leaves and seeds	Leaves and seeds	"
OCT. Seeds are available well into winter		

Best-tasting parts: Leaves.

Use: Raw or cooked. Mild flavor. In salads, soups, sauces, omelets, and lasagne. Seeds are also edible. They can be lightly roasted and ground into flour or cooked as hot cereal. Seeds can also be sprouted.

Look-alikes: When immature–many, including squaw paint (edible).
When mature–amaranth (edible), saltbrush (edible), poison suckleya (toxic; not common).

Caution: Do not eat rank smelling or bad tasting *Chenopodium* family members, and, like spinach, eating large quantities of lambs quarter may produce mild oxalate/nitrate poisoning.

Note: You have pulled this ubiquitous weed from your lawns and gardens a thousand times.

LICORICE MINT *(Agastache foeniculum var. anethiodora)*

Other names: Licorice hyssop mint

Altitude: 4,000–8,000 feet.

Description: Perennial. Herbaceous. Aromatic. Ornamental. Height to 30 inches. Stems are square. Opposite leaves. Flowers are a purplish terminal spike, about 1 to 3-inches tall. Licorice mint is found growing in groups or solitary. It dies back to ground level each winter. Leaves turn yellow in autumn.

Macrohabitat: The northern half of our region. Not very common.

Microhabitat: Canyon bottoms, meadows; partial shade. Damp soil.

Plant Growth Phases		
Lower Altitudes	**Middle Altitudes**	**Higher Altitudes**
APRIL	Sprouting	Dormant	Rare
MAY	Stem, leaf growth	Sprouting	"
JUNE	Flower buds	Stem, leaf growth	"
JULY	Flowering	Flower buds	"
AUG.	Flowering	Flowering	"
SEPT.	Seedheads	Seedheads	"
OCT.	Dried leaves on the plant are flavorful until Dec.		"

Best-tasting parts: Leaves.

Use: Anise flavored. Use in salads, soups, sauces, candy, and as licorice flavoring. Lightly steeped for tea. Dried leaves retain flavor for a long time.

Look-alikes: When immature–many.
              When mature–other mint family members.

Note: Sweet cicely (edible), is another licorice/anise flavored wild plant found in the Rockies at higher altitudes.

MALLOW *(Malva neglecta var. rotundifolia)*

Other names: Common mallow, cheese weed, dwarf mallow.

Altitude: 4,000–8,500 feet.

Description: Annual or biennial. Herbaceous. Low spreading. Height to 12 inches. Roundish leaves up to 4-inches wide, have scalloped edges. Flowers are small, ⅜ to ½-inch wide, cup-shaped, and usually pink or white (rarely blue). Fruit is a round, pie-sectioned structure, ½ inch in diameter. Mallow is found growing in dense groups or solitary. It dies back to ground level each winter.

Macrohabitat: Very common in our region, mostly below 7,000 feet.

Microhabitat: Disturbed soil; near human habitation.

Plant Growth Phases		
Lower Altitudes	**Middle Altitudes**	**Higher Altitudes**
APRIL	Sprouting	Sprouting	Rare
MAY	Leaf growth	Leaf growth	"
JUNE	Flowering	Flowering	"
JULY	Flowering/fruits	Flowering	"
AUG.	Flowering/fruits	Flowering/fruits	"
SEPT.	Flowering/fruits	Flowering/fruits	"
OCT.	Frost damage	Frost damage	"

Best-tasting parts: Leaves, flowers, and fruits.

Use: Mild flavor. Great in salads, marinades, omelets, casseroles, and as a soup thickener. The mild flavor permits liberal use of mallow in any dish.

Look-alikes: When immature–young red currant (edible fruit), thimbleberry (edible fruit), hollyhock.
        When mature–none.

Note: A species related to mallow was used to manufacture marshmallows at one time.

MILKWEED *(Asclepias speciosa)*

Other names: Silkweed, showy milkweed, milk plant, butterflyweed, wild cotton, lecheros.

Altitude: 4,000–8,500 feet.

Description: Perennial. Coarse. Stout. Milky Sap. Height to 4 feet. Oval leaves are leathery, with a large pink midrib. Showy flower clusters, usually pinkish, are 2 to 4-inches wide. Seedpods look like fat okra pods with course hairs/bumps. Milkweed is found growing solitary or in clumps (less than 10 stems per clump). It dies back to ground level each winter.

Macrohabitat: Throughout our region; numerous below 7,000 feet.

Microhabitat: Roadsides, fencerows, fields, valley floors. Damp-to-dry soil.

Plant Growth Phases			
	Lower Altitudes	**Middle Altitudes**	**Higher Altitudes**
APRIL	Sprouting	Dormant	Rare
MAY	Stem, leaf growth	Sprouting	"
JUNE	Flower buds/flowers	Stem, leaf growth	"
JULY	Flowering	Flowering	"
AUG.	Seedpods	Seedpods	"
SEPT.	Seedpods dry out	Seedpods dry out	"
OCT.	Seeds blow away	Seeds blow away	"

Best-tasting parts: Flower buds, flowers, and young pods.

Use: Raw or cooked. Salads, soups, omelets, stir-fries, kebabs. Even if the outer pod hull is too dry late in the season, the inner parts may still be moist and edible. In the spring, young milkweed shoots are also edible, but are difficult to identify and not recommended for beginners. (See "Look-alikes" section below.)

Look-alikes: When immature–dogbane (toxic), and other *Asclepias spp.*
When mature–none (poison milkweed is a distant look-alike. It has white or cream-colored flowers, narrow grass-like leaves, whorled around the stem, and a more slender, smoother pod).

Note: A few authors report that milkweed is poisonous when fresh, but I have eaten small quantities fresh many times without ill effects. It is best to be cautious anyway. As with all wild edibles, eat only small amounts at first. (See "Identification" section in the Introduction.)

ONION—Nodding Flowers *(Allium cernuum)*

Other names: Nodding onion, nodding garlic, wild onion.

Altitude: 5,000–11,000 feet.

Description: Perennial. Herbaceous. Xerophytic. Aromatic. Height to 2 feet. A few grass-like, sometimes fleshy leaves. Flowers are pink, sometimes white, in umbels, 1 to 3-inches across. Stems curve downward (nodding) at the tip. Seeds are small, in tan capsules, eventually splitting open. Root sheaths are red or white. Nodding onion usually grows clumped together, eight plantlets or less. It is sometimes solitary in widespread communities. Onions die back to ground level each winter.

Macrohabitat: Common throughout our region, below 10,000 feet.

Microhabitat: Anywhere, especially sunny, rocky hillsides. Damp-to-dry soil.

Plant Growth Phases			
	Lower Altitudes	**Middle Altitudes**	**Higher Altitudes**
APRIL	Sprouting	Dormant	Dormant
MAY	Leaf growth	Sprouting	Dormant
JUNE	Flowering	Leaf growth	Sprouting
JULY	Flowering/seeds	Flowering	Leaf growth
AUG.	Umbel seedpods	Flowering/seeds	Flowering
SEPT.	Pods split open	Pods split open	Flowering/seeds
OCT.	Identify the dried, brown, umbel seed structure and enjoy onion root even in winter.		

Best-tasting parts: Roots, leaves, flowers.

Use: All parts of the onion are edible if they are not too tough. Great in salads, omelets, and as a garnish. Cooked in casseroles, stir-fries, or steamed. Pickled onion relish is also good.

Look-alikes: When immature—many (some toxic; see "Caution" below). When mature—other onion family members. (See High Altitude section.)

Caution: Safest onion harvest time is during flowering. Make sure your plant smells like onion before eating. Only onions smell like onions. Death camas (see Toxic Plants) looks like onion before flowering. (When harvesting, make sure you are not smelling onion scent on your fingers from previous picking, while sniffing death camas.)

Note: The sulphur compounds found in the onion/garlic family of plants have been found to be very healthful for us.

PENNYCRESS *(Thlaspi arvense)*

Other names: Field pennycress, garlic mustard, pennycress mustard.

Altitude: 4,000–10,000 feet.

Description: Annual. Herbaceous. Weedy. Height, 6 to 20 inches. Leaves in a basal rosette form early, 1 to 4-inches long. The flower stem is branching or not. Upper stem leaves are smaller, clasping. White 4-petal flowers are in a raceme "squirrel-tail" form (see Glossary), with the youngest on top, seedpods developing below, and the most mature at the bottom. Seedpods are flat, round, with wings, ¼ to ½-inch wide, and looking like peppergrass seedpods, but larger. Seeds are small, and dark brownish-red. Pennycress usually grows solitary or in dispersed groupings, and dies back to ground level each winter. Like many plants, it is generally smaller at higher altitudes. Pennycress will often produce a second crop of young plants in August and September.

Macrohabitat: Common throughout our region below 9,000 feet.

Microhabitat: Fields, disturbed soil, around human habitation.

Plant Growth Phases		
Lower Altitudes	**Middle Altitudes**	**Higher Altitudes**
APRIL Sprouting	Sprouting	Dormant
MAY Flowering	Flowering	Sprouting
JUNE Flowering/seedpods	Flowering/seedpods	Flowering
JULY Seedpods	Seedpods	Flowering/seedpods
AUG. Seedpods	Seedpods	Seedpods
SEPT. Seedpods	Seedpods	Seedpods
OCT. Many seeds available until December		

Best-tasting parts: Leaves and seeds.

Use: Strong, almost garlic-like flavor. Older leaves are more bitter. Young fresh leaves work best in salads, sauces, soups, and stir-fries (a little goes a long way). Seeds may be ground into flour, or used whole as a flavoring or topping on bagels and breads. Seeds can also be sprouted.

Look-alikes: When immature–many.
When mature–Peppergrass (edible; has smaller seedpods).

Caution: Wild mustards have been known to cause intestinal irritation when eaten to excess.

Note: In the temperate zones, humans have developed a somewhat symbiotic relationship with the mustard family of plants. They provide us with very healthful vegetables (i.e. broccoli, cauliflower, cabbage, wild mustards), and we provide them with the disturbed soil around our homes that they thrive in.

PEPPERGRASS *(Lepidium spp.)*

Other names: Pepper mustard, field cress, cow cress.

Altitude: 4,000–10,000 feet.

Description: Annual or perennial. Herbaceous. Xerophytic. Weedy. Some species are woody at the base when mature. Height, 8 to 40 inches. Some exhibit a bush form (like a tumbleweed). Leaves, 1 to 4-inches long, form a basal rosette early, then dry up by mid-season. Flower stems are usually branching. Upper stem leaves are smaller and clasping. The tiny whitish flowers are in racemes (typical mustard "squirrel-tail" form; see Glossary), with the youngest on top, seedpods developing below, and oldest at bottom. Seedpods are small, round, with wings, and look like pennycress seedpods, but smaller. Peppergrass is found growing solitary or in dispersed groupings, and it dies back to ground level each winter. It is generally smaller at higher altitudes. Peppergrass will often produce a second crop of young plants in August and September.

Macrohabitat: Common throughout, but mostly below 9,000 feet.

Microhabitat: In fields, disturbed soil; around human habitation.

Plant Growth Phases		
Lower Altitudes	**Middle Altitudes**	**Higher Altitudes**
APRIL Sprouting	Sprouting	Dormant
MAY Stem, leaf growth	Stem, leaf growth	Sprouting
JUNE Flowering	Flowering	Stem, leaf growth
JULY Flowering	Flowering	Flowering
AUG. Flowering/seedpods	Flowering/seedpods	Flowering/seedpods
SEPT. Seedpods	Seedpods	Seedpods

Best-tasting parts: Leaves and seeds.

Use: Spicy-hot or peppery flavor. Use in salads, sauces, soups, and salsa. Roasted seeds may be ground into a spicy flour. Overcooking reduces spiciness. Seeds can also be sprouted.

Look-alikes: When immature–many.
When mature–pennycress (edible; has larger seedpods).

Caution: Wild mustards have been known to cause intestinal irritation when eaten to excess.

Note: A few peppergrass species have a bad taste. Avoid these. They are not toxic, just inedible.

PEPPERMINT (Mentha arvensis, M. canadensis)

Other names: Poleo mint, field mint, Canada mint, creek mint.

Altitude: 4,000–10,000 feet.

Description: Perennial. Herbaceous. Aromatic. Water-loving. Height to 3 feet. Opposite leaves. Square stems are thin, weak, sometimes branching. Flower clusters on the upper stem are purple-pink, and in leaf axils. They are about ½-inch across, developing into seed structures lower on the stem, with the most mature toward the bottom. Peppermint grows solitary or sometimes in tight colonies, and dies back to ground level each winter.

Macrohabitat: Common throughout our region.

Microhabitat: Always in or near a water source. Damp-to-wet soil.

Plant Growth Phases			
	Lower Altitudes	**Middle Altitudes**	**Higher Altitudes**
APRIL	Sprouting	Dormant	Dormant
MAY	Stem, leaf growth	Sprouting	Dormant
JUNE	Flowering	Stem, leaf growth	Sprouting
JULY	Flowering	Flowering	Stem, leaf growth
AUG.	Flowering/seeds	Flowering/seeds	Flowering
SEPT.	Flowering/seeds	Flowering/seeds	Flowering/seeds
OCT.	Dried leaves can be found on branches until about Dec.		

Best-tasting parts: Leaves and stems.

Use: Tea, sauce, gelatin, meat flavoring, ice cream, mint jelly, salads, and as a garnish. Dry leaves for tea.

Look-alikes: When immature–many.
　　　　　　　　When mature–spearmint.

Note: If it is found wild in our region, mint scented, and has a square stem, it is safe to eat. Also, the mint family is well known for treating mild stomach upset or nausea.

PIN CHERRY *(Prunus pensylvanica var. corymbulosa)*

Other names: Bird cherry, fire cherry, wild red cherry.

Altitude: 5,000–9,500 feet.

Description: Perennial. Arborescent. Deciduous. Small tree/shrub. Height to 10 feet. Dark bark, reddish twigs, and leaves 2 to 6-inches long with small teeth around their edges. The white flowers are ¾-inch wide, and in clusters. Fruit is red when ripe, ¼ inch in diameter, with a single, hard seed. Pin cherry grows in loose groupings or solitary. Autumn leaf colors are usually red or orange.

Macrohabitat: Sparsely distributed throughout our region. It is smaller at higher altitudes.

Microhabitat: Creekbanks, rocky slopes, burn areas.

Plant Growth Phases		
Lower Altitudes	**Middle Altitudes**	**Higher Altitudes**
APRIL Leaves emerge	Dormant	Rare
MAY Flowering	Leaves emerge	"
JUNE Unripe fruit	Flowering	"
JULY Unripe fruit	Unripe fruit	"
AUG. Ripe fruit	Ripe fruit	"
SEPT. Ripe fruit	Ripe fruit	"

Best-tasting parts: Fruits (cherries).

Use: Acid-sour cherries are mixed with other fruits to make gelatin, juice, jam, fruit leather, syrup, and pemmican. Screen out seeds.

Look-alikes: When immature–chokecherry, plum, serviceberry (all with edible fruit).

When mature–chokecherry (edible fruit).

Note: Pin cherry is not an abundant fruit producer in our region. Also, like all wild fruits, it is vulnerable to extreme weather conditions during flowering in the spring. Late frosts or too much rain may decrease the fruit crop later. And, like many commercial fruits, the seeds of pin cherry are mildly poisonous.

PIÑON PINE *(Pinus edulis)*

Other names: Nut pine.

Altitude: 4,000–9,000 feet.

Description: Perennial. Arborescent. Evergreen. Xerophytic. Ornamental. Bushy pine tree. Height, 15 to 20 feet. The needles are 1 to 2-inches long, usually two together. Cones are 1 to 2½-inches long, and ¾ to 1¾-inches in diameter. Cone seeds are egg-shaped, wingless, and about 1/2-inch long. Piñon usually grows solitary, in dispersed communities.

Macrohabitat: Common in our southwestern regions, below 8,000 feet.

Microhabitat: Rocky, dry soil. Foothills, mesas, desert areas. Usually growing with juniper and ponderosa pine.

Plant Growth Phases		
Lower Altitudes	**Middle Altitudes**	**Higher Altitudes**
APRIL Unripe cones	Unripe cones	Rare
MAY "	"	"
JUNE "	"	"
JULY "	"	"
AUG. "	"	"
SEPT. Harvest full-size cones in autumn when just about to open		

Best-tasting parts: Nuts.

Use: Good raw or roasted. Place closed cones in 350-degree oven to facilitate opening. Roasting piñon nuts improves their flavor and provides for longer storage. Remove shells and use with any recipe requiring nuts. Also, nut butter, soup thickener, stir-fries, candy, and ash cakes. Tea can be made from the leaves of all pines in the Rockies.

Look-alikes: When immature–other pine family members.
When mature–other pine family members.

Note: Growth is very slow. Cones take years to develop. There seems to be a good crop every 3 to 7 years. Be mindful of the sticky sap when harvesting. Also, there is speculation that a large, wild stand of piñon pine growing in northern Colorado, hundreds of miles from its normal range, was planted by Native Americans many years ago.

PLUM *(Prunus americana var. ignota)*

Other names: Wild plum, American plum.

Altitude: 4,000–7,000 feet.

Description: Perennial. Deciduous. Xerophytic. Shrubby. Height to 15 feet (typically 5 to 7 feet). Pseudo-spiny. Small-toothed leaves are 2 to 4-inches long. Flowers are in white clusters, rarely pink. Individual flowers are about 1-inch wide. Plum is found flowering profusely in the spring while the leaves are still small. Fruit is round or oval, about 1 inch in diameter, red, purple, or orange, with one large, hard seed. Plum often forms tight thickets; it is rarely solitary. Autumn leaf colors are red or orange.

Macrohabitat: Found throughout our region; mostly lower altitudes.

Microhabitat: Canyon bottoms, valleys, fencerows, lower hillsides. Medium-moist-to-dry soil.

Plant Growth Phases		
Lower Altitudes	**Middle Altitudes**	**Higher Altitudes**
APRIL Flowering	Dormant	Rare
MAY Flowering	Flowering	"
JUNE Young green fruits	Flowering/green fruits	"
JULY Unripe fruits	Unripe fruits	"
AUG. Ripe fruits	Ripe fruits	"
SEPT. Few fruits	Few fruits	"
OCT. A few dried fruits are available on the branches into winter		

Best-tasting parts: Only the fruits (plums).

Use: Sour flavor. Good in jelly, sauce, wine, gelatin, juice, fruit leather, and syrup. May be dehydrated.

Look-alikes: When immature–chokecherry and pin cherry (both have edible fruit). When mature–sand cherry (*P. besseyi* is only found on the eastern boundaries of our region. It is also edible).

Note: After planting a 12-inch tall wild plum seedling on my property at 7,000 feet, it took 10 years to produce its first fruit. Flowers and young fruits are susceptible to frost and excessive moisture in the spring, affecting fruit production later. Also, like many commercial fruits, the seeds of plum are poisonous.

PRICKLY PEAR *(Opuntia spp.)*

Other names: Beavertail cactus, Indian fig, tuna, altuna.

Altitude: 4,000–8,000 feet.

Description: Perennial. Succulent. Evergreen. Ornamental. Xerophytic. Height to 30 inches. Flat, jointed, fleshy stems are without leaves, looking like a beaver's tail. Many spines and bristles. Flowers are large, 2 to 5-inches, and yellow, orange, or red. Fruit is on top of the stems, usually red, and juicy when ready to harvest. Fruit is also spiny, and contains many small seeds. Prickly pear is usually found growing together in clumps, or is sometimes solitary.

Macrohabitat: Throughout our area, but the really succulent fruited species are found in the southern and eastern regions of the Rockies.

Microhabitat: Anywhere sunny, dry, rocky, and/or sandy. Most abundant below 6,000 feet.

Plant Growth Phases		
Lower Altitudes	**Middle Altitudes**	**Higher Altitudes**
APRIL	Flower buds begin	Dormant	Rare
MAY	Flowering	Flower buds begin	"
JUNE	Flowering	Flowering	"
JULY	Unripe fruits	Flowering	"
AUG.	Ripe fruits	Unripe fruits	"
SEPT.	Ripe fruits	Ripe fruits	"
OCT.	Few ripe fruits left. Fleshy stems available year-round		

Best-tasting parts: Fruits.

Use: Burn off the large spines. The tiny spines don't burn off, so peel the outer skin with a knife. Fruits are used for jelly, syrup, sauce, fruit leather, gelatin, or wine. Screen out the seeds. Fruits may be dried. Fleshy stems are also edible. Fry sliced stems for sandwiches (remove spines as mentioned above). Seeds may be roasted and ground into flour.

Look-alikes: When immature–none.
When mature–none.

Caution: It is difficult to remove all tiny spines, called glochids. It is not dangerous if a few are eaten accidentally. Butter will help remove glochids from skin.

Note: Some larger prickly pear clumps may be over 100 years old. Do not harvest from these. Also, many people think the prickly pear pads are leaves. They are actually modified stems.

PURSLANE *(Portulaca oleracea)*

Other names: Common purslane, common portulaca, verdolagas.

Altitude: 4,000–8,500 feet.

Description: Annual. Succulent. Weedy. Low spreading. Height to 8 inches or less. Fleshy stems (up to 24-inches long), and oval leaves (up to ¾-inch long). Small, yellow flowers are ¼ inch in diameter. Tiny seeds. A matting growth habit is exhibited with larger specimens. Purslane stays tender and succulent as it matures, unlike many other wild edible plants. It is found growing solitary or together, and purslane dies back to ground level each winter.

Macrohabitat: Throughout our region, mostly below 7,000 feet.

Microhabitat: As a weed, it can be found anywhere, in damp-to-dry soil.

Plant Growth Phases			
	Lower Altitudes	**Middle Altitudes**	**Higher Altitudes**
APRIL	Sprouting	Dormant	Rare
MAY	Stem/leaf growth	Sprouting	"
JUNE	Flowering	Stem/leaf growth	"
JULY	Flowering	Flowering	"
AUG.	Continued flowering and leaf growth		"
SEPT.	Continued flowering and leaf growth		"
OCT.	Frost damage renders it unusable after a while		"

Best-tasting parts: Leaves and succulent stems.

Use: May be used raw or cooked. Somewhat sour tasting when young. Good as a soup thickener, marinade, steamed, pickled, in casseroles, and fresh on sandwiches. The tiny seeds are edible and may be roasted, ground into flour, or sprouted.

Look-alikes: When immature–kinnikinnik (edible fruit; tougher stems and leaves), creeping amaranth (edible).
When mature–kinnikinnik (edible fruit; tougher stems and leaves), creeping amaranth (edible).

Caution: Like spinach, eating excessive quantities of purslane may lead to mild oxalate poisoning.

Note: Purslane resists drying, but it may be dehydrated for later use by scalding briefly in boiling water before laying out to dry. This will speed up the drying process.

RED CURRANT *(Ribes cereum)*

Other names: Wax currant, squaw currant.

Altitude: 4,000–11,500 feet.

Description: Perennial. Woody shrub. Deciduous. No spines. Height to 6 feet. Leaves are roundish, and ½ to 1½-inches wide. Flowers are pink, sometimes white, and tube-shaped, ¼ to ½-inch long. Fruit is round, red, somewhat translucent, usually smooth, and with a persistent dried flower attached. Seeds are soft. Red currant grows as a solitary bush with others close by.

Macrohabitat: Very common throughout our region. Best fruit yields are below 9,000 feet.

Microhabitat: Anywhere sunny. Damp-to-dry soil.

Plant Growth Phases		
	Lower Altitudes	**Middle Altitudes**	**Higher Altitudes**
APRIL	Leaves show	Dormant	Dormant
MAY	Flowering	Leaves/flowering	Dormant
JUNE	Green fruits	Flowering	Leaves/flowering
JULY	Ripe fruits	Green fruits	Flowering
AUG.	Ripe fruits	Ripe fruits	Green/ripe fruits
SEPT.	Few fruits left	Ripe fruits	Ripe fruits
OCT.	Some dried fruits are available on the branches through the winter		

Best-tasting parts: Flowers and fruits.

Use: The fresh flowers are good in wildflower salads, fruit salads, as a garnish, or cooked. The fruits don't taste like other currants, but work well in pies, pastries, puddings, and jam (alone, or mixed with other fruits). May be dehydrated.

Look-alikes: When immature–mallow (edible), thimbleberry (edible fruit), hollyhock, nine-bark.

　　　　　When mature–none.

Note: All currants (except some of the hi-bush currants) display the persistent, pronounced dried spindle on the fruit (see photo). This is the remnant of the earlier spring flower. This feature makes currant easy to identify. Of all the currants, the red currant is the most prolific fruit producer in the Rockies.

SALMONBERRY *(Rubus parviflorus)*

Other names: Thimbleberry, Japanese raspberry.

Altitude: 4,000–10,000 feet.

Description: Perennial. Woody shrub. No spines. Deciduous. Height to 5 feet. Large, five-lobed leaves are up to 8-inches wide. Flowers are white and 1 to 1½-inches wide. Fruit is green, then reddish. Seeds are soft. Salmonberry fruit looks like raspberry, but it is less juicy. It grows in communities; rarely solitary.

Macrohabitat: Erratic in distribution. Most common between 6,000–9,000 feet in the mountains.

Microhabitat: Shady, moist forest. Creek banks. North slopes.

Plant Growth Phases			
	Lower Altitudes	**Middle Altitudes**	**Higher Altitudes**
APRIL	Leaves emerge	Dormant	Dormant
MAY	Flowering	Leaves emerge	Dormant
JUNE	Young fruit	Flowering	Leaves emerge
JULY	Unripe fruit	Young fruit	Flowering
AUG.	Ripe fruit	Unripe/ripe fruit	Unripe fruit
SEPT.	Some ripe fruit	Ripe fruit	Ripe fruit
OCT.	The few dried fruits on the stems lose flavor quickly		

Best-tasting parts: Fruits.

Use: Like raspberries, but not as moist, salmonberry is good in pies, preserves, syrup, gelatin, or mixed with other fruits. May be dehydrated to preserve.

Look-alikes: When immature–thimbleberry (*R. deliciosus*), squashberry, and grape (all edible).
When mature–thimbleberry (*R. deliciosus*, edible).

Note: An edible orange or yellow-berried variety (*R. spectabilis*) may be found in our northwestern regions (smaller leaves). The common name "thimbleberry" is used for both *R. parviflorus* and *R. deliciosus* (both edible) in our region (see "Thimbleberry").

SALSIFY (Tragopogon pratensis, T. dubius, T. porrifolius)

Other names: Oyster root, goatsbeard, wild salsify.

Altitude: 4,000–11,000 feet.

Description: Biennial or perennial. Herbaceous. Weedy. Milky sap. Height to 3 feet. Taproot. In the first year, leaves are clasping; grass-like. The second year, single flowers appear, usually yellow, sometimes purple (*T. porrifolius*), 1 to 2-inches wide, on partly hollow stems. Seeds have parachutes. Seedhead looks like a dandelion seedhead, but larger, 3 to 4-inches wide. Salsify is found growing solitary. It dies back to ground level each winter.

Macrohabitat: Widespread and very common, mostly below 9,000 feet. The purple-flowered variety is more common in our southern regions.

Microhabitat: Fields, meadows; anywhere sunny. Damp-to-dry soil.

Plant Growth Phases (Second year growth)		
Lower Altitudes	**Middle Altitudes**	**Higher Altitudes**
APRIL Grass-like leaves	Dormant	Dormant
MAY Flower stalk begins	Grass-like leaves	Dormant
JUNE Flowering	Flower stalk begins	Grass-like leaves
JULY Flowering/seedheads	Flowering	Flower stalk begins
AUG. Flowering/seedheads	Flowering/seedheads	Flowering
SEPT. Flowering/seedheads	Flowering/seedheads	Flowering/seedheads
OCT. Flowering rare; most seedheads blown away		

Best-tasting parts: Roots (before flower stalk appears).

Use: Harvest first-year roots, or second-year before the flower stalk appears (it is difficult to identify at these times); otherwise, the root is too tough and bitter. The root tastes somewhat like oysters when cooked, especially the purple-flowered variety. It is best in a white sauce over pasta. Also good in stew, chowder, and gumbo.

Look-alikes: When immature–many (some toxic; not recommended for beginners). When mature–none.

Note: Salsify is a popular commercial crop in some parts of the world.

SALTBRUSH *(Atriplex spp.)*

Other names: Orache, spearscale, saltbush.

Altitude: 4,000–9,000 feet.

Description: Annual. Herbaceous. Height to 4 feet. Some branching possible. Leaves are arrow-head shaped and 1 to 6-inches wide. Flowers are in greenish clumps on the upper stems, and inconspicuous. Saltbrush often has many small seeds. It is usually found growing solitary, with others in the area. Saltbrush dies back to ground level each winter.

Macrohabitat: Throughout our region; mostly below 8,000 feet.

Microhabitat: Sunny, open areas. Growing in a variety of soils, especially alkali and salt flats, medium-moist-to-dry.

Plant Growth Phases			
	Lower Altitudes	**Middle Altitudes**	**Higher Altitudes**
APRIL	Sprouting	Dormant	Rare
MAY	Stalk, leaf growth	Sprouting	"
JUNE	Green flowers	Stalk, leaf growth	"
JULY	Green flowers	Green flowers	"
AUG.	Seeds	Green flowers	"
SEPT.	Seeds	Seeds	"
OCT.	The edible leaves are available from sprouting to well into autumn		

Best-tasting parts: Leaves (especially top leaves).

Use: Slight salty flavor, particularly during dry years. Fresh in salads, salad dressings, pesto, tacos, guacamole, or cooked in omelets, rice pilaf, nettle soup, egg rolls, quiche, lasagne, vegie-burgers, and as fritters. The seeds are also edible roasted, ground into flour, or sprouted. The ashes of the burned leaves after drying are used as a salt substitute.

Look-alikes: When immature–lambs quarter (edible), poison suckleya (toxic; not common).
When mature–lambs quarter (edible).

Note: Many shrubby (woody) varieties also belong to this group; more common in our southwestern regions. They are used similarly.

SERVICEBERRY *(Amelanchier alnifolia, A. pumila, A. utahensis)*

Other names: Juneberry, shadberry, sarvisberry, saskatoonberry, shadblow.

Altitude: 5,000–11,000 feet.

Description: Perennial. Arborescent. Deciduous. Woody shrub, or small tree. Height to 20 feet (usual height 4 to 10 feet). Bark is usually purplish colored and smooth with no spines. Leaves are roundish to oblong, toothed at the tip, smooth at the base, and 1 to 3-inches long. White flowers are in clusters. Each flower is about ¾-inch wide. Fruit is green, then reddish-purple, then dark blue. Seeds are soft. Serviceberry looks a bit like a blueberry. It can be found forming thickets or solitary. Fruit production is minimal at higher altitudes.

Macrohabitat: Throughout our area. More common in northern regions, and below 9,000 feet. Dwarf specimens above 9,000 feet.

Microhabitat: Canyon floors; mountainsides. Moderately moist soil.

Plant Growth Phases			
	Lower Altitudes	**Middle Altitudes**	**Higher Altitudes**
APRIL	Leaves emerge	Dormant	Dormant
MAY	Flowering	Leaves emerge	Dormant
JUNE	Green, unripe fruits	Flowering	Leaves emerge
JULY	Ripe fruits	Green, unripe fruits	Flowering
AUG.	Ripe fruits	Ripe fruits	Green/ripe fruits
SEPT.	Fruits dwindle	Ripe fruits	Ripe fruits
OCT.	Most fruit gone	Most fruit gone	Most fruit gone

Best-tasting parts: Fruit.

Use: The flavor is not real strong, but is good mixed with other fruits in jam, pies, smoothies, strawberry shortcake, fruit compote, fruit leather, dumplings, and pemmican. May be dried for preservation.

Look-alikes: When immature–hawthorn, (edible fruit).
                When mature–hawthorn, (edible fruit).

Note: This tree was named by 19th century undertakers from the north country. In the spring, when the serviceberry was flowering, they knew the ground had finally thawed enough to dig graves again.

SOLOMONSEAL *(Smilacina stellata)*

Other names: Star solomonseal, solomonplume, false solomonseal, wild lily of the valley, starflower.

Altitude: 4,000–10,000 feet.

Description: Perennial. Herbaceous. Height to 2 feet. Unbranched stem with alternate, non-toothed leaves, folded at the midrib, lance-shaped, and parallel veined, 2 to 8-inches long. White flowers are in a zigzag raceme, have six petals, and are about ¼-inch wide. Fruit is green with black longitudinal stripes, then red, purple, or (rarely) gold, ¼ inch in diameter. Several seeds. Solomonseal is found growing in colonies; occasionally solitary. It dies back to ground level each winter.

Macrohabitat: Common throughout our region.

Microhabitat: Shady or sunny areas. Damp-to-moist soil.

Plant Growth Phases			
	Lower Altitudes	**Middle Altitudes**	**Higher Altitudes**
APRIL	Sprouting	Dormant	Dormant
MAY	Flowering	Sprouting	Dormant
JUNE	Unripe fruit	Flowering	Sprouting
JULY	Ripe fruit	Unripe fruit	Flowering
AUG.	Ripe fruit	Ripe fruit	Unripe fruit
SEPT.	Few fruits left	Ripe fruit	Ripe fruit
OCT.	Fruit gone	Few fruits left	Few fruits left

Best-tasting parts: Ripe fruit.

Use: The curious flavor is good for pancake syrup, sauce, pies, cake icing, jelly, fruit compote, candy, and fruit leather. Boil fruits, screen out seeds, then mix with other fruits. The young shoots are edible as well.

Look-alikes: When immature–many, including false hellebore (toxic; larger, more stout); solomonplume, twisted stalk, fairy bells (all three with edible fruit). When mature–baneberry (toxic), solomonplume (edible).

Caution: Some authors have reported laxative effects, probably when fruits were eaten to excess.

Note: Solomonseal roots exhibit small patterns, or "seals," hence the name solomonseal; however, the plant does not need to be uprooted for identification.

SPEARMINT *(Mentha spicata)*

Other names: Field mint, yerba buena.

Altitude: 4,000–9,000 feet.

Description: Perennial. Herbaceous. Aromatic. Height to 3 feet. Stem is square, often branching, with opposite leaves up to 3-inches long. Light bluish-purple flowers grow in terminal spikes or leaf axils. Spearmint grows in colonies or solitary; it dies back to ground level each winter.

Macrohabitat: Throughout our region, but not common in the wild.

Microhabitat: Drainages. Creek beds. Moist-to-wet soil.

Plant Growth Phases			
	Lower Altitudes	**Middle Altitudes**	**Higher Altitudes**
APRIL	Sprouting	Dormant	Rare
MAY	Leaves available	Sprouting	"
JUNE	Leaves available	Leaves available	"
JULY	Flowering	Leaves available	"
AUG.	Flowering	Flowering	"
SEPT.	Flowering/seeds	Flowering/seeds	"
OCT.	Dried leaves on stems available and flavorful until about Dec.		

Best-tasting parts: Leaves, tender stems.

Use: Iced tea, mint juleps, vegetable or fruit salads, jelly, sauce, candy, ice cream, gelatin, and as a flavoring or garnish. Flowers are also edible. Spearmint may be dried for preservation.

Look-alikes: When immature—stinging nettle (edible after cooking or drying), figwort, and other mint family members.
   When mature—other mint family members.

Note: If it is mint-scented, with a square stem, and found wild in our region, it is safe to eat. Also, spearmint may be propagated easily from seed or root stock in shady, damp areas.

SQUAWBUSH *(Rhus trilobata)*

Other names: Three-leaf sumac, limonada, skunkbush.

Altitude: 4,000–9,000 feet.

Description: Perennial. Deciduous. Xerophytic. Aromatic. Spineless, woody shrub. Height to 6 feet. Leaves are made up of three leaflets, each looking somewhat like a mitten. The flower is small, ⅛ inch in diameter, yellow/cream colored, and grows in a cluster. Flowers usually bloom before the leaves appear, making squawbush easy to identify in the spring. Fruit clusters are green, then red, and sticky. The berry is hard. Autumn leaf colors are orange and red. Squawbush usually grows solitary with others in the area.

Macrohabitat: Very common throughout our region; most common below 7,000 feet.

Microhabitat: Foothills, mesas, dry rocky soil.

Plant Growth Phases		
Lower Altitudes	**Middle Altitudes**	**Higher Altitudes**
APRIL Dormant	Dormant	Rare
MAY Flowering	Flowering	"
JUNE Leaves fill in	Leaves fill in	"
JULY Green fruits	Green fruits	"
AUG. Ripe, red fruits	Ripe, red fruits	"
SEPT. Ripe fruits	Ripe fruits	"
OCT. Many fruits stay on the branches into the winter		

Best-tasting parts: Fruits.

Use: Fruits are hard and sour. Lightly steep berries for sour tea, or use as a lemon juice substitute in guacamole, gelatin, or whenever a lemon-sour flavor is required. Fruits are abundant. Similar in use to sumac.

Look-alikes: When immature–none.
When mature–none.

Note: Squawbush stems are good for basketmaking, and the leaves were reportedly used as a tobacco substitute.

STINGING NETTLE *(Urtica dioica var. procera, U. gracilenta)*

Other names: Nettle.

Altitude: 4,000–10,000 feet.

Description: Perennial. Herbaceous. Erect. Stinging hairs. Height to 6 feet. Toothed leaves are opposite on somewhat square stems. Flowers are in green clusters growing from leaf axils, and eventually turn into brown seed clusters. Stinging nettle dies back to ground level each winter, and grows in tight groups or solitary.

Macrohabitat: Throughout our region, more common below 8,000 feet.

Microhabitat: Canyon floors, often shady sites. Damp soil.

Plant Growth Phases		
Lower Altitudes	**Middle Altitudes**	**Higher Altitudes**
APRIL Sprouting	Dormant	Dormant
MAY Leaf, stalk growth	Sprouting	Sprouting
JUNE Flower clusters begin	Leaf, stalk growth	Leaf, stalk growth
JULY Flowering	Flower clusters begin	Flower clusters begin
AUG. Seed production	Flowering	Flowering
SEPT. Seeds	Seeds	Seeds
OCT. The edible foliage is available to first frost		

Best-tasting parts: Young, leafy stem tops and leaves. (Do not eat raw!)

Use: Harvest carefully or with gloves. Cooking or thorough drying eliminates the sting. Cook in omelets, casseroles, stuffing, egg rolls, quiche, crepes, and nettle-onion soup. Can also be used as a rennet substitute in cheesemaking.

Look-alikes: When immature–many.
When mature–figwort, and mint family members.

Note: As it is related to hemp, the stem fibers of stinging nettle make good cordage or twine. Also, stinging nettle and poison ivy are the two most common "contact" poisonous plants in the Rocky Mountains.

SUMAC *(Rhus glabra)*

Other names: Smooth sumac, scarlet sumac, dwarf sumac.

Altitude: 4,000–7,500 feet.

Description: Perennial. Arborescent. Deciduous. Ornamental. Height to 20 feet (usual height, 3 to 6 feet). Smooth bark is sometimes fuzzy when new. Leaves are compound; leaflets are lance-shaped, 2 to 5-inches long. Flower clusters near the top growth have tiny, whitish flowers that mature into hard, red pyramidal berry clusters. Individual berries are similar to squawbush berries. Autumn leaf colors are red. Sumac forms thickets and it is rarely found growing solitary.

Macrohabitat: Throughout our region, mostly in foothill zones.

Microhabitat: Canyon bottoms, creek banks, woodland borders. Damp-to-moderately dry soil.

Plant Growth Phases			
	Lower Altitudes	**Middle Altitudes**	**Higher Altitudes**
APRIL	Leaves emerge	Dormant	Rare
MAY	Leaf growth	Leaves emerge	"
JUNE	Flowers	Flowers	"
JULY	Unripe fruit	Unripe fruit	"
AUG.	Ripe fruit	Ripe fruit	"
SEPT.	Ripe fruit	Ripe fruit	"
OCT.	Fruit is available on the branches through the winter; flavor decreases with time		

Best-tasting parts: Red fruits.

Use: Bruise ripe fruit clusters and lightly steep to make sour tea, or use as a lemon juice substitute in guacamole, gelatin, or wherever a lemon/sour flavor is required (similar in use to squawbush). Harvest before rain leaches away the sour flavor.

Look-alikes: When immature–red elder (toxic), greenes mountain ash, New Mexico locust (toxic), and mesquite (edible).
When mature–red elder (toxic), greenes mountain ash.

Note: This small tree is a popular landscape tree in our region, and most people don't realize that the fruits are edible.

TANSY MUSTARD *(Descurainia sophia)*

Other names: Flixweed.

Altitude: 4,000–9,000 feet.

Description: Annual or biennial. Herbaceous. Weedy. Height to 3 feet. Usually branched. Leaves are highly dissected and delicate looking. Flowers are tiny and yellow, with four petals. Seedpods are in the typical mustard "squirrel-tail" form (see Glossary), flowering on top, with seedpod growth below; oldest are at the bottom. Individual seedpods are narrow and up to 1-1/2-inches long. Seeds are brown and tiny. Tansy mustard grows in colonies or solitary, and dies back to ground level each winter.

Macrohabitat: Throughout our region; mostly below 8,000 feet.

Microhabitat: Sun or partial shade. Disturbed ground. Medium-moist-to-dry soil.

Plant Growth Phases			
	Lower Altitudes	**Middle Altitudes**	**Higher Altitudes**
APRIL	Flowering	Sprouting	Rare
MAY	Flowering	Flowering	"
JUNE	Flowering/seedpods	Flowering	"
JULY	Flowering/seedpods	Flowering/seedpods	"
AUG.	Seedpods	Seedpods	"
SEPT.	Seedpods	Seedpods	"
OCT.	Seeds may be harvested until about Nov.		"

Best-tasting parts: Leaves.

Use: Leaves are mildly spicy, but somewhat dry textured, so it is best to combine them with others, fresh, in salads. Cook in stir-fries, casseroles, soups, omelets, bean dishes, and quiche. Excessive cooking reduces spiciness. Also, seeds are edible and sproutable.

Look-alikes: When immature–many, including corydalis and poison hemlock (toxic).
        When mature–other mustard family members.

Caution: Wild mustards have been known to cause intestinal irritation when eaten to excess.

Note: The wild edible mustards have been growing in disturbed soil around the world for thousands of years. How many long winter famines were ended by the early sprouting of this healthful family of plants?

THIMBLEBERRY *(Rubus deliciosus)*

Other names: Boulder raspberry, Rocky Mountain raspberry.

Altitude: 4,000–10,000 feet.

Description: Perennial. Woody shrub. No spines. Height and width to 6 feet. Peeling older bark contrasts with the fuzzy, reddish new bark. Flowers are white, showy, and 1 to 3-inches wide, with five petals. Leaves are roundish and three- or five-lobed. Whitish fruit turns purplish-translucent when ripe. Thimbleberry usually grows as a solitary shrub. Autumn leaf colors are yellow.

Macrohabitat: Throughout our foothills. Common below 8,000 feet.

Microhabitat: Sunny, rocky locations. Moderate-to-dry soil.

Plant Growth Phases		
	Lower Altitudes	**Middle Altitudes**	**Higher Altitudes**
APRIL	Leaves emerge	Dormant	Dormant
MAY	Flowering	Leaves, flowering	Leaves emerge
JUNE	Unripe fruit	Flowering	Flowering
JULY	Ripe fruit	Unripe/ripe fruit	Flowering
AUG.	Most fruit gone	Ripe fruit	Unripe/ripe fruit
SEPT.	Fruit gone	Most fruit gone	Ripe fruit
OCT.	Fruit gone	Fruit gone	Fruit gone

Best-tasting parts: Fruit.

Use: Fruit is sweet, juicy, and seedy, but becomes mushy when harvested. It is best to use it quickly and mix with other fruits in smoothies, pies, pudding, strudel, cookies, jam, wine, syrup, gelatin, ice cream, fruit leather, and crepes.

Look-alikes: When immature–currants (edible fruits).
When mature–none.

Note: The name "thimbleberry" is also used for *Rubus parviflorus* (see "Salmonberry").

TOMATILLO *(Physalis spp.)*

Other names: Husk tomato, ground cherry, popweed.

Altitude: 4,000–8,000 feet.

Description: Annual or perennial. Herbaceous. Height to 3 feet. Stems are covered with oval or oblong leaves. Flowers are usually yellow, sometimes purple, and ½ to 1-inch wide. Fruit is a berry inside a papery husk. Seeds are small and white. Tomatillo grows in colonies or solitary, and dies back to ground level each winter.

Macrohabitat: Throughout the Rockies; less common in northern and western regions.

Microhabitat: Open, sunny areas. Moderate soil moisture.

Plant Growth Phases			
	Lower Altitudes	**Middle Altitudes**	**Higher Altitudes**
APRIL	Sprouting	Dormant	Rare
MAY	Leaf growth	Sprouting	"
JUNE	Flowering	Leaf growth	"
JULY	Flowering	Flowering	"
AUG.	Fruits ripen	Fruits ripen	"
SEPT.	Ripe fruits	Ripe fruits	"
OCT.	Some dried fruits on the stem are available into the winter		

Best-tasting parts: Fruit (do not eat the leaves).

Use: Raw, cooked, or dried. Fresh tomatillo fruit is good in salads or as a garnish. Cooked, it is good in pies, salsa, pudding, kebabs, syrup, fruit leather, and pastries. The dried fruit tastes like dried apricots/raisins. Use dried fruits in cookies or cereal.

Look-alikes: When immature–many, including mullein and houndstongue.
When mature–none.

Note: Tomatillo is in the nightshade family, as are domestic tomatoes and potatoes, all with poisonous foliage.

TUMBLEMUSTARD *(Sysimbrium altissimum)*

Other names: Jim Hill mustard.

Altitude: 4,000–8,500 feet.

Description: Annual or biennial. Herbaceous. Weedy. Height and width to 6 feet. A basal rosette of leaves appears early, then becomes multi-branched. Stem leaves and basal leaves often dry up and fall off by August. Flowers have four petals, ½-inch wide, yellow, sometimes white, or rarely purple. Seedpods are narrow, 1 to 3-inches long, and look like small branches. Seeds are tiny and brown. Ultimately, the larger tumblemustards look somewhat like a mature tumbleweed. When mature, tumblemustard does not seem to display the obvious "squirrel-tail" pattern often observed in other edible mustards. Found growing in groups or solitary, it dies back to ground level each winter.

Macrohabitat: Throughout our region. Very common.

Microhabitat: Usually open areas; disturbed soil. Damp-to-dry soil.

Plant Growth Phases			
	Lower Altitudes	**Middle Altitudes**	**Higher Altitudes**
APRIL	Flower stalk begins	Rosette of leaves	Sprouting
MAY	Flowering	Flower stalk begins	Rosette of leaves
JUNE	Flowering	Flowering	Flower stalk begins
JULY	Flowering	Flowering	Flowering
AUG.	Reaches full size	Full size	Flowering
SEPT.	Seedpods	Seedpods	Seedpods
OCT.	Seeds can be harvested into the winter		

Best-tasting parts: Leaves.

Use: Raw or cooked. Mildly spicy, it is good fresh in salads, sandwiches, and tacos. Cooked, use it in soups, sauces, rice pilaf, omelets, egg rolls, casseroles, chili, and potato salad. Seeds can be roasted and ground into flour or sprouted.

Look-alikes: When immature–many, including dandelion (edible).
             When mature–tumbleweed (edible).

Caution: Wild mustards have been known to cause intestinal irritation when eaten to excess.

Note: This is the plant that gave us the phrase, "Too old to cut the mustard." It originated from railroad laborers in the 1800s, hired to hand-cut weeds off railroad tracks in the mountains and deserts of the West.

WATERCRESS *(Rorippa nasturtium-aquaticum)*

Other names: Cress, pepperleaf.

Altitude: 4,000–8,000 feet.

Description: Perennial. Aquatic. Stems floating or trailing. Height to 6 inches. Compound leaves of 3 to 9 leaflets. Each leaflet is oval-shaped and 1 to 1½-inches long. Numerous flowers are white with four petals, and ½-inch wide. Fruit, a slender pod, is ½ to 1½-inches long, and slightly curved. Watercress exhibits a short mustard "squirrel-tail" form (see Glossary). Matting growth habit; rarely solitary.

Macrohabitat: Throughout; common at lower altitudes.

Microhabitat: In or near a water source. Wet soil or mud.

Plant Growth Phases			
	Lower Altitudes	**Middle Altitudes**	**Higher Altitudes**
APRIL	Leaves	Dormant	Rare
MAY	Flowering	Leaves emerge	"
JUNE	Flowering/seedpods	Flowering	"
JULY	Flowering/seedpods	Flowering/seedpods	"
AUG.	Flowering wanes	Flowering/seedpods	"
SEPT.	Mostly seedpods	Mostly seedpods	"
OCT.	Some leaves and stems available for harvesting		"

Best-tasting parts: Leaves, stems.

Use: Peppery flavored. Watercress may be used fresh in salads, sandwiches, cole slaw, tacos, marinade, and herb butter. (Rinse thoroughly.) Cooked, use it in soups, omelets, casseroles, potato salad, and rice dishes.

Look-alikes: When immature–water hemlock (very poisonous; see Toxic Plants). When mature–none.

Note: Edible leaves and stems are often available for harvesting year-round during mild winters at lower altitudes. The word "cress" indicates a member of the mustard family of plants.

WOOD SORREL *(Oxalis stricta, O. violacea)*

Other names: Sourgrass.

Altitude: 4,000–8,500 feet.

Description: Annual or perennial. Herbaceous. Small. Height to 8 inches. Leaves, green or purple, with three heart-shaped leaflets, ¼ to ½-inch wide. Flowers are five-petaled and mostly yellow, but can sometimes be violet, pink, or white. The banana-shaped fruit is ½-inch long, and pops open when disturbed. Wood sorrel is found growing in colonies or solitary. It dies back to ground level each winter.

Macrohabitat: *O. stricta* is common throughout our region; *O. violacea* is more common in southern regions.

Microhabitat: Sunny meadows; forest borders. Usually rich damp soil. Can be found growing underneath existing vegetation.

Plant Growth Phases			
	Lower Altitudes	**Middle Altitudes**	**Higher Altitudes**
APRIL	Sprouting	Dormant	Rare
MAY	Flowering	Sprouting	"
JUNE	Flowering	Flowering	"
JULY	Flowering	Flowering	"
AUG.	Flowering/seedpods	Flowering/seedpods	"
SEPT.	Seedpods	Seedpods	"
OCT.	Frost damage	Frost damage	"

Best-tasting parts: Leaves, flowers, fruits.

Use: With its sour flavor, wood sorrel is best when used fresh in salads, as a lemon-substitute garnish on steamed trout, in cottage cheese, sandwiches, omelets, rice dishes, and fruit salads. Lightly cooked, it may be used in soups and sauces; or lightly steeped, as a tea.

Look-alikes: When immature–clover (edible).
　　　　　　　When mature–none.

Caution: Like spinach, eating very large quantities of wood sorrel may lead to mild oxalate poisoning.

Note: This is a tiny plant difficult to spot, but easy to propagate from seed. It is one of our three great sour-tasting sorrels in the Rockies. Upon handling the seedpods, the tiny seeds will pop out. Some may think they are small, hopping bugs.

YUCCA *(Yucca spp.)*

Other names: Spanish bayonet, soapweed, datil, amole.

Altitude: 4,000–8,000 feet.

Description: Perennial. Xerophytic. Ornamental. Evergreen. Height to 5 feet. Stiff, spine-tipped, lance-like leaves are clustered near the base in a rosette pattern, and reach up to 30-inches long, ½ to 3-inches wide. The stalk, ¼ to 1½-inches wide, supports showy, off-white fleshy flowers, 2 to 4-inches wide, with six petal-like segments, becoming an oval green fruit, 2 to 8-inches long. The seeds are usually black. Yucca grows together in clumps or solitary.

Macrohabitat: Throughout our region; less common up north.

Microhabitat: Sunny, rocky, dry plains, slopes. Damp-to-dry soil.

Plant Growth Phases			
	Lower Altitudes	**Middle Altitudes**	**Higher Altitudes**
APRIL	Stalk sprouts	Dormant	Rare
MAY	Flowering	Stalk sprouts	"
JUNE	Flowering	Flowering	"
JULY	Fruit growth	Flowering	"
AUG.	Seeds ripen	Fruit growth	"
SEPT.	Seeds ripe	Seeds ripe	"
OCT.	Seeds ripe	Seeds ripe	"

Best-tasting parts: Flower buds, flowers, and young fruits.

Use: Raw or cooked. Buds and flowers work well in soups, salads, omelets, kebabs, fritters, or stir-fries. Young fruits can be sliced and fried, baked, stuffed, barbecued, or pickled. Dehydrate to preserve. Seeds may be roasted and ground into flour. Some people report a disagreeable aftertaste and/or laxative effect with this plant.

Look-alikes: When immature–none.
                 When mature–none.

Note: A needle and thread can be made for emergency sewing by partially cutting off the spine tip, but leaving attached some of the long leaf fibers. Also, Yucca's leaves are good cordage fibers; soap may be made from its roots; and the dried stalk can be used as the spindle in friction firestarting.

HI-BUSH CURRANT *(Ribes spp.)*

Other names: Prickly currant, Colorado currant, sticky currant.

Altitude: 7,500–11,500 feet.

Description: Perennial. Deciduous. Woody shrub. Height to 5 feet. Branches are either spiny or spineless. Leaves are roundish in outline, lobed or not, and 1 to 5-inches wide. Flowers, tubular or saucer-shaped, are white, green, pink, or purple. Fruit, with soft prickles or smooth, is black or red, and about ¼ inch in diameter. The persistent, pronounced, dried flower parts on the fruit (like other currants) are usually nonexistent. The hi-bush currant grows either in thickets or as a solitary shrub.

Macrohabitat: Throughout our region; common at higher altitudes.

Microhabitat: Canyons, mountainsides. Some species like shade, some like sun. Some like dry soil, but most hi-bush currants like a more moist soil.

Plant Growth Phases			
	Lower Altitudes	**Middle Altitudes**	**Higher Altitudes**
APRIL	Rare	Leaves emerge	Dormant
MAY	"	Flowering	Leaves emerge
JUNE	"	Flowering	Flowering
JULY	"	Unripe fruits	Flowering
AUG.	"	Ripe fruits	Unripe/ripe fruits
SEPT.	"	Ripe fruits	Ripe fruits
OCT.	"	Few dried fruits on branches into winter	

Best-tasting parts: Fruits.

Use: Alone, or mixed with other fruit in jams, pies, fruit salad, pancakes, fruit leather, ash cakes, syrup, crepes, or with just cream and sugar. Can be dehydrated.

Look-alikes: When immature–other currants.
When mature–other currants.

Note: The lack of a persistent, pronounced dried flower part on the fruit (like other currants) makes identification more difficult for the novice.

HUCKLEBERRY *(Vaccinium myrtillus, V. caespitosum, V. scoparium)*

Other names: Blueberry, dwarf huckleberry, bilberry, grouseberry, whortleberry.

Altitude: 8,000–12,000 feet.

Description: Perennial. Deciduous. Small, shrubby and low growing to a height of 12 inches or less. No spines. Small leaves are about 1-inch long, with tiny teeth around the leaf edges. Flowers, usually pink and/or white, are urn-shaped, and ¼-inch long. Fruit is black, blue, or red, and less than ½ inch in diameter. Seeds are small and soft. Huckleberry is found growing in colonies (sometimes as a ground cover) or solitary.

Macrohabitat: More abundant in the northern regions. Upper montane, sub-alpine, and alpine altitudinal zones.

Microhabitat: Aspen/spruce/lodgepole forest floors, north facing slopes, burn areas, acidic soil. Not found in dry soil.

Plant Growth Phases			
	Lower Altitudes	**Middle Altitudes**	**Higher Altitudes**
APRIL	Rare	Dormant	Dormant
MAY	"	Leaf buds open	Dormant
JUNE	"	Flowering	Leaf buds open
JULY	"	Green, unripe fruits	Flowering
AUG.	"	Ripe fruits	Green to ripe fruits
SEPT.	"	Ripe fruits	Ripe fruits
OCT.	"	No fruits	No fruits

Best-tasting parts: Berries.

Use: Huckleberries taste like commercial blueberries, but they are usually smaller. They can be used in jam, syrup, wine, pemmican, cold or hot cereal, and more. Dry for preservation. It can be tedious to collect large quantities.

Look-alikes: When immature–many.
When mature–none.

Note: This is my favorite wild berry, and can be found during high altitude hikes in August and September. It is the crème de la crème of wild berries!

KINNIKINNIK (Arctostaphylos uva ursi)

Other names: Bearberry, Uva ursi, creeping manzanita, chipmunk apples, hog cranberry, coralillo.

Altitude: 6,000–10,000 feet.

Description: Perennial. Evergreen. Ornamental. Ground cover. Height, 6 inches or less. Woody stems have shreddy, peeling bark. Shiny, oval, leathery leaves are 1-inch long or less. Small, white and pink urn-shaped flowers are ¼-inch long. Fruit is shiny green, then bright red when ripe, and ¼ inch in diameter, with a few hard seeds. Slow growing with a matting growth habit, kinnikinnik is almost never solitary.

Macrohabitat: Frequent throughout the mountains of our region. Most common between 7,000 and 9,000 feet.

Microhabitat: Rocky ground, poor soil, burn areas, open clearings in pine/aspen forests.

Plant Growth Phases			
	Lower Altitudes	**Middle Altitudes**	**Higher Altitudes**
APRIL	Rare	Evergreen leaves	Evergreen leaves
MAY	"	Flowering	Evergreen leaves
JUNE	"	Young green berries	Flowering
JULY	"	Green berries	Young green berries
AUG.	"	Red, ripe berries	Green berries
SEPT.	"	Red, ripe berries	Red, ripe berries
OCT.	"	Many berries available through the winter under the snow	

Best-tasting parts: Raw berries do not have a great flavor (dry, astringent, and seedy). Cooking brings out the sweet flavor.

Use: Boil fruits to make sauce, jelly, syrup, gelatin, and tea. Add other fruit. Screen out the seeds. Dehydrated berries last many years. Dried leaves are used as tobacco and for a tanning agent.

Look-alikes: When immature—purslane (edible, succulent), wintergreen (edible). When mature—wintergreen (edible).

Note: The word "kinnikinnik" has Native American origins and was probably used by many western tribes for thousands of years. It is usually translated to mean "tobacco mixture." Bears will often eat a lot of these berries before going into hibernation.

MOUNTAIN SORREL *(Oxyria digyna)*

Other names: Alpine sorrel, round-leaf sorrel.

Altitude: 8,000–13,000 feet.

Description: Perennial. Herbaceous. Height to 16 inches. Fleshy leaves are round, heart, or kidney shaped, ½ to 1½-inches wide, and sometimes colored purple from frost. Inconspicuous flowers become seeds on a green/red stalk. Seeds have wings. Grows in very dispersed colonies or solitary. This plant dies back to ground level each winter.

Macrohabitat: Throughout our region; most numerous around timberline.

Microhabitat: Subalpine and alpine fields. Damp areas among rocks, ledges, and crevices.

Plant Growth Phases			
	Lower Altitudes	**Middle Altitudes**	**Higher Altitudes**
APRIL	Rare	Dormant	Dormant
MAY	"	Sprouting	Dormant
JUNE	"	Leaf growth	Sprouting
JULY	"	Flowering (inconspicuous)	Leaf growth
AUG.	"	Winged seeds	Flowering (inconspicuous)
SEPT.	"	Leaves still edible	Winged seeds
OCT.	"	Leaves are edible until frost damage in Nov.	

Best-tasting parts: Leaves.

Use: Sour flavor. Use on sandwiches, in salads, cottage cheese, or as a lemon substitute garnished on fish. Lightly cooked in soups, sauces, and omelets, it still retains some sourness. Try fermenting with watercress, sauerkraut-style.

Look-alikes: When immature–none.
When mature–none.

Caution: Like spinach, eating very large amounts of mountain sorrel could lead to mild oxalate poisoning.

Note: The leaves of mountain sorrel, sheepsorrel, and wood sorrel all have that wonderful sour flavor!

ONION–Red or Pink Flowers (Allium brevistylum, A. geyeri, A. acuminatum, A. sibericum)

Other names: Short-styled onion, geyer onion, hookers onion, Siberian chive.

Altitude: 4,500–12,000 feet.

Description: Perennial. Herbaceous. Xerophytic. Aromatic. Height from 6 to 40 inches. Root sheaths are fibrous or not. Grass-like, sometimes fleshy leaves. Flowers are red or pink, in erect umbels, 1 to 2½ inches in diameter. Seeds are in small capsules. Grows clumped together, or solitary in dispersed communities. Onions die back to ground level each winter.

Macrohabitat: Abundant within its altitudinal zone.

Microhabitat: Anywhere. Wet-to-dry soil.

Plant Growth Phases			
	Lower Altitudes	**Middle Altitudes**	**Higher Altitudes**
APRIL	Sprouting	Dormant	Dormant
MAY	Flowering	Sprouting	Dormant
JUNE	Flowering	Flowering	Sprouting
JULY	Seed structures	Flowering	Flowering
AUG.	Dried seed stalk	Seed structures	Flowering
SEPT.	Dried seed stalk	Dried seed stalk	Seed structures
OCT.	Recognizing the dried umbel seed structure during winter yields an edible root		

Best-tasting parts: Roots, leaves, flowers.

Use: All parts of the onion are edible if they're not too tough. Try it cooked in potato-onion pancakes, vegie-burgers, pasta sauce or onion-nettle soup. (see "stinging nettle").

Look-alikes: When immature–many (some toxic; see "Caution" below). When mature–other onion family members.

Caution: Safest onion harvest time is during flowering. Make sure your plant smells like onion before eating. Only onions smell like onions. Death camas (see Toxic Plants) looks like onion before flowering. (When harvesting, make sure you are not smelling onion scent on your fingers from picking, while sniffing death camas.)

Note: The onions with dark pink-colored flowers seem to have the strongest flavor.

ONION–White Flowers *(Allium geyeri, A. textile, A. brandegei)*

Other names: Geyer onion, white onion, wild onion.

Altitude: 4,000–12,000 feet.

Description: Perennial. Herbaceous. Xerophytic. Aromatic. Height from 6 to 40 inches. Root sheaths are usually fibrous. Grass-like, sometimes fleshy leaves. Flowers are white, in erect umbels, 1 to 2½ inches in diameter. Seeds are in small capsules. These onions are found growing clumped together, or solitary, in dispersed communities. They die back to ground level each winter.

Macrohabitat: Abundant. More common at lower altitudes.

Microhabitat: Anywhere. Medium-moist-to-dry soil.

Plant Growth Phases			
	Lower Altitudes	**Middle Altitudes**	**Higher Altitudes**
APRIL	Few flowers	Sprouting	Dormant
MAY	Flowering	Flowering	Sprouting
JUNE	Flowering	Flowering	Flowering
JULY	Seed structures	Seed structures	Flowering
AUG.	Dried seed stalk	Dried seed stalk	Flowering/seeds
SEPT.	Dried seed stalk	Dried seed stalk	Seed structures
OCT.	Recognizing the dried, umbel seed structure through winter yields an edible root		

Best-tasting parts: Roots, leaves, flowers.

Use: Many uses. Chopped fresh in homemade salad dressing, chip dip, and on sandwiches. Cooked in sauces, soups, and on bagels.

Look-alikes: When immature–many (some toxic; see "Caution" below). When mature–other onion family members.

Caution: Safest onion harvest time is during flowering. Make sure your plant smells like onion before eating. Only onions smell like onions. Death camas (see Toxic Plants) looks like onion before flowering. (When harvesting, make sure you are not smelling onion scent on your fingers from picking, while sniffing death camas.)

Note: The wild onion is one of the most abundant wild edible plants during the growing season, and it is the most abundant wild plant food available during our Rocky Mountain winters.

RASPBERRY *(Rubus idaeus var. strigosus)*

Other names: American red raspberry.

Altitude: 5,000–11,500 feet.

Description: Perennial. Deciduous. Shrub-like growth habit. Height to 6 feet. Mostly woody stems; bristly or prickly. Leaflets, 3 to 5 together, are 1 to 3-inches long, green above, lighter below. Flowers are green-white, ½ inch in diameter. Fruit is whitish, then red, and about ½ inch in diameter. Soft seeds. Found growing in tight thickets or solitary. Autumn leaf colors are dark red, purple, or yellow.

Macrohabitat: Widely distributed throughout our region up to timberline.

Microhabitat: Anywhere, except very wet or very dry soil.

Plant Growth Phases			
	Lower Altitudes	**Middle Altitudes**	**Higher Altitudes**
APRIL	Leaves emerge	Dormant	Dormant
MAY	Flowering	Leaves emerge	Dormant
JUNE	Unripe fruits	Flowering	Leaves emerge
JULY	Ripe fruits	Unripe fruits	Flowering
AUG.	Ripe fruits	Ripe fruits	Unripe fruits
SEPT.	Most fruit gone	Ripe fruits	Ripe fruits
OCT.	Most fruit gone	Most fruit gone	Most fruit gone

Best-tasting parts: Berries.

Use: Great in cold or hot cereal, fresh fruit cocktail, crepes, pastries, cobblers, pies, smoothies, preserves, syrup, and more.

Look-alikes: When immature–none.
When mature–none.

Note: Black raspberries look virtually identical, but for black fruit, and they are scattered in our region. Blackberries are rare in the Rockies.

ROSE (Rosa spp.)

Other names: Wild rose, mountain rose.

Altitude: 4,000–11,000 feet.

Description: Perennial. Prickly, woody shrub. Deciduous. Ornamental. Height to 8 feet. Stems and twigs are reddish. Showy, five-petaled, pinkish flowers are 1½ to 2½-inches wide. Leaves are compound. Small, toothed leaflets. Fruit (hip) is green, then red, ¼ to ¾ inch in diameter, with small, hard seeds. Found growing as a dense thicket, or a solitary shrub.

Macrohabitat: Less common at lower altitudes in our southern regions; otherwise, widespread and common.

Microhabitat: Forest and field. Mountain and plain. Medium-moist soil.

Plant Growth Phases			
	Lower Altitudes	**Middle Altitudes**	**Higher Altitudes**
APRIL	Leaves emerge	Dormant	Dormant
MAY	Flowering	Leaves emerge	Leaves emerge
JUNE	Flowering	Flowering	Flowering
JULY	Green hips	Flowering	Flowering
AUG.	Red, ripe hips	Green hips	Green hips
SEPT.	Red, ripe hips	Red, ripe hips	Red, ripe hips
OCT.	Red-colored hips are available through the winter		

Best-tasting parts: Fruits (hips).

Use: Raw, they are somewhat tasteless, but boiled, they make good jelly, fruit butter, and wine. Blend with other fruit for fruit leather, syrup, or cookies. Screen out the seeds. Dry hips for preservation, tea, or to grind into powder, seed and all. The flower petals are also edible and tea may be made from the dried leaves.

Look-alikes: When immature–gooseberry and raspberry (both edible). When mature–none.

Note: Fresh, ripe rose hips are the most potent wild source of vitamin C in the Rockies. One rose hip is equal to about 500 mg of vitamin C. Drying and heating deplete the vitamin C in the hips.

SEDGE *(Cyperaceae)*

Other names: Flatsedge, spikesedge, spikerush, bulrush.

Altitude: 4,000–12,000 feet.

Description: Perennial. Herbaceous. Height up to 10 feet, but most are under 2 feet. Grass-like plants usually having triangular stems, no stem joints or nodes, and flower/seed structures that are often spike-like on the upper stem. Flowers are inconspicuous. Many have leaves with small, sharp teeth along leaf edges. Found growing either in colonies or solitary.

Macrohabitat: Throughout our region; very common.

Microhabitat: Wet places. Bogs. Marshes. In or near a water source. Some members of this large family grow in drier soil, but the most plentiful seed harvest will be from wet areas.

Plant Growth Phases		
	Lower Altitudes	**Middle Altitudes**	**Higher Altitudes**
APRIL	Small leaves	Small leaves	Dormant
MAY	Flowering	Flowering	Leaves sprout
JUNE	Immature seeds	Immature seeds	Flowering
JULY	Immature seeds	Immature seeds	Immature seeds
AUG.	Seeds harvestable	Seeds harvestable	Seeds harvestable
SEPT.	Seeds harvestable	Seeds harvestable	Seeds harvestable
OCT.	Some seeds are harvestable into the winter months		

Best-tasting parts: Seeds (grain).

Use: Roasted seeds are ground into flour and mixed with other flours for use in breads, cakes, pancakes, seedcakes, ash cakes, flatbreads, nut loaf, or cooked as a hot cereal.

Look-alikes: When immature–many (some toxic).

When mature–grasses (all grass seeds without ergot fungi are edible, but they should be winnowed and roasted well before grinding into flour, as some have spiny chaff).

Note: Bulrush (large, cylindrical stems) is included in this large plant family, and is often found growing with cattails. Bulrush offers edible seeds and roots.

SHEEPSORREL *(Rumex acetosella)*

Other names: Sorrel, sourgrass, red sorrel, lemon plant.

Altitude: 4,000–11,500 feet.

Description: Perennial. Herbaceous. Height to 2 feet but usually much less. Leaves are arrowhead shaped, 1 to 6-inches long, with pronounced basal lobes. Flowers are green and inconspicuous at first, then flowers/seedheads turn reddish. Tiny seeds. Grows in patches or solitary. (Difficult to find if growing solitary.)

Macrohabitat: Throughout; common.

Microhabitat: Sunny meadows. Open areas. Medium-moist soil.

Plant Growth Phases			
	Lower Altitudes	**Middle Altitudes**	**Higher Altitudes**
APRIL	Small leaves	Small leaves	Dormant
MAY	Green flowers	Leaves	Small leaves
JUNE	Reddish flowers	Green flowers	Leaves
JULY	Reddish seed stalks	Reddish flowers	Green flowers
AUG.	Reddish seed stalks	Reddish seed stalks	Reddish flowers
SEPT.	Reddish seed stalks	Reddish seed stalks	Reddish seed stalks
OCT.	Small, green leaves can be found year-round at ground level, lower/middle altitudes		

Best-tasting parts: Leaves.

Use: Sour flavor. Fresh leaves are excellent in salad, cottage cheese, omelets, rice pilaf, fruit salad, and as a garnish on cooked fish. Cooking or drying diminishes the flavor.

Look-alikes: When immature–bindweed.
　　　　　　　When mature–none.

Caution: Like spinach, eating very large quantities of sheepsorrel may lead to mild oxalate poisoning.

Note: This is the most abundant of all the great sour tasting sorrels. (See mountain sorrel and wood sorrel.)

SOLOMONPLUME *(Smilacina racemosa)*

Other names: False solomonseal, wild lily of the valley.

Altitude: 6,500–10,500 feet.

Description: Perennial. Herbaceous. Height to 3 feet. Single, arching stem (no branching). Slight zigzag pattern to the stem. Leaves are alternate, parallel veined, clasping the stem, have a pointed oval shape, and are 2 to 8-inches long. Flowers are off-white, in a raceme up to 8-inches long. Fruit is light colored with tiny red spots, then all red, ⅛ to ¼ inch in diameter. A single seed, ⅛ inch or less. Grows in groups or solitary. Solomonplume dies back to ground level each winter.

Macrohabitat: Throughout our mountainous regions.

Microhabitat: Deep forests, creeksides, some meadows. Rich, damp soil.

Plant Growth Phases			
	Lower Altitudes	**Middle Altitudes**	**Higher Altitudes**
APRIL	Rare	Dormant	Dormant
MAY	"	Sprouting	Sprouting
JUNE	"	Flowering	Flowering
JULY	"	Unripe fruit	Unripe fruit
AUG.	"	Ripe, red fruit	Unripe fruit
SEPT.	"	Ripe fruit	Ripe, red fruit
OCT.	"	Most fruit gone	Most fruit gone

Best-tasting parts: Berries.

Use: The relatively large seed sometimes limits the use of the fresh fruit, but it is cooked for jelly, sweet sauces, puddings, syrup, gelatin, glaze, and pastries. Screen out the seeds. The young sprouts are also edible. (See "Look-alikes" below.)

Look-alikes: When immature–many, including false hellebore (toxic), solomonseal (edible), twisted stalk (edible), fairy bells (edible).
          When mature–baneberry (toxic; see Toxic Plants), solomonseal (edible).

Caution: Some people have reported laxative effects upon eating large quantities of solomonplume berries.

Note: Solomonplume is related to solomonseal and twisted stalk, all with red-colored edible berries.

SQUASHBERRY *(Vibernum edule, var. pauciflorum)*

Other names: Hi-bush cranberry, mooseberry.

Altitude: 6,000–10,000 feet.

Description: Perennial. Deciduous. Woody shrub with no spines. Height to 6 feet. Opposite leaves. The leaves look somewhat like grape or maple leaves, 1 to 5-inches wide. White flowers are in clusters, 1 to 3-inches across. Sparse fruits are green, then dull red, then bright red when ripe, ¼ to ½ inch in diameter, and contain a single, flat seed. Autumn leaf colors are red. Squashberry is often found growing in widespread groups or solitary.

Macrohabitat: Not very common, but most common at the higher altitudes.

Microhabitat: Canyon floors; shady, moist woodlands; along creeks.

Plant Growth Phases			
	Lower Altitudes	**Middle Altitudes**	**Higher Altitudes**
APRIL	Rare	Leaf buds	Leaf buds
MAY	"	Leaves emerge	Leaves emerge
JUNE	"	Flowering	Flowering
JULY	"	Green fruits	Green fruits
AUG.	"	Unripe, red fruits	Unripe, red fruits
SEPT.	"	Ripe fruits	Ripe fruits
OCT.	"	Dried fruits on the stem through the winter	

Best-tasting parts: Fruit.

Use: Tart, acidic berries taste like cranberries. Mix them with other fruits and cook for a wild cranberry sauce, syrup, jelly, fruit leather, or anything requiring a cranberry flavor. Screen out the seeds. It is usually difficult to collect an abundance of these fruits.

Look-alikes: When immature–grape, thimbleberry (both with edible fruits), maple. When mature–none.

Note: A wild cranberry sauce made from squashberries is guaranteed to complement that special Thanksgiving meal.

SQUAW PAINT *(Chenopodium capitatum, C. overi)*

Other names: Strawberry blite, Indian paint.

Altitude: 6,000–11,000 feet.

Description: Annual. Herbaceous. Height up to 2 feet. Leaves are 1 to 3-inches long, arrowhead shaped, and often have small lobes at the leaf base. Stems are erect, leaning, or arched; branching or not. Flowers are inconspicuous in green spike-like clusters, or axillary clusters, then turn bright red, looking like a raspberry. Seeds are small and brown. Usually solitary plants.

Macrohabitat: Widespread throughout our region.

Microhabitat: Canyon and valley floors. Rocky, moist-to-damp soil. Disturbed soil.

Plant Growth Phases		
Lower Altitudes	**Middle Altitudes**	**Higher Altitudes**
APRIL Sprouting, rosette	Sprouting, rosette	Dormant
MAY Leaf growth	Leaf growth	Sprouting, rosette
JUNE Green flower clusters	Green flower clusters	Leaf growth
JULY Clusters turn red	Clusters turn red	Green flower clusters
AUG. Red clusters (fruits)	Red clusters (fruits)	Clusters turn red
SEPT. Clusters dry out	Clusters dry out	Red clusters (fruit)
OCT. Frost damage	Frost damage	Frost damage

Best-tasting parts: Red, berrylike clusters are mildly sweet.

Use: Raw or cooked. Fresh in vegetable or fruit salads, or as a showy garnish. Cooked in omelets, fruit compote, crepes, or lightly steamed. Also, edible sprouts from seeds, and leaves are edible.

Look-alikes: When immature–other *Chenopodium* family members. When mature–none.

Note: A beautiful plant when ripe, squaw paint may be propagated from seed quite easily.

STONECROP *(Sedum lanceolatum var. stenopetalum)*

Other names: Yellow stonecrop, orpine.

Altitude: 5,000–13,000 feet.

Description: Perennial. Succulent. Xerophytic. Sometimes evergreen. Height to 8 inches. Leaves are whorled around stem; fleshy. Yellow flowers on top of the stems have five petals. Fruit is a small brown capsule. Leaves are purplish-brown during winter. Found in loose groupings or solitary.

Macrohabitat: Widespread in our mountainous zones. Very common.

Microhabitat: Sunny, rocky locations. Dry, rocky soil.

Plant Growth Phases		
Lower Altitudes	**Middle Altitudes**	**Higher Altitudes**
APRIL Succulent leaves	Succulent leaves	Few leaves
MAY Flowering begins	Succulent leaves	Few leaves
JUNE Flowering	Flowering begins	Succulent leaves
JULY Flowers dwindle	Flowering	Flowering begins
AUG. Succulent leaves	Flowers dwindle	Flowering
SEPT. Succulent leaves	Succulent leaves	Flowers dwindle
OCT. Succulent leaves	Succulent leaves	Succulent leaves

Best-tasting parts: Flowers, stems, and leaves. Best when flowering. Very juicy, with a mild flavor.

Use: Raw or cooked. Fresh in all-flower salads, tacos, omelets, cole slaw, or pickled. Cooked in egg rolls, soups, pizza, burritos, stir-fries, quiche, meat loaf and nut loaf.

Look-alikes: When immature–queens crown (edible), kings crown (edible). When mature–none.

Note: This *Sedum* family member has adapted to drought by storing water in its leaves and stems, thus giving it that moist, juicy texture when eaten.

STRAWBERRY *(Fragaria spp.)*

Other names: Wild strawberry, earth mulberry.

Altitude: 4,000–11,500 feet.

Description: Perennial. Herbaceous. Small, low plants. Often spreading by reddish runners. Height less than 8 inches. Leaves with three, toothed leaflets. Flowers, five-petaled, are white with yellow centers. The ripe, red fruit has tiny seeds embedded on its surface. Usually grows in colonies; occasionally solitary. Autumn leaf colors are red or yellow.

Macrohabitat: Common throughout our region, especially at higher altitudes.

Microhabitat: Meadows; open or shady locations. Damp soil. Look for it under existing vegetation.

Plant Growth Phases			
	Lower Altitudes	**Middle Altitudes**	**Higher Altitudes**
APRIL	Sprouting	Dormant	Dormant
MAY	Flowering	Sprouting	Dormant
JUNE	Fruits ripen	Flowering	Sprouting
JULY	Fruits ripe	Fruits ripen	Flowering
AUG.	Fruits dwindling	Fruits ripe	Fruits ripen
SEPT.	Few fruits left	Few fruits left	Fruits dwindle
OCT.	Most fruit gone	Most fruit gone	Most fruit gone

Best-tasting parts: Fruit.

Use: Fresh in fruit salads, smoothies, frozen yogurt, or strawberry shortcake. Cooked in pies, puddings, turnovers, jam, gelatin, fruit leather, fruit butter, syrup, crepes, and pastries. Tea can be made from the fresh or dried leaves.

Look-alikes: When immature–some *Potentilla* members (yellow flowers when mature).
When mature–none.

Note: Once you find one ripe strawberry fruit, look around, and you'll probably find more.

SWEET CICELY *(Osmorhiza spp.)*

Other names: Anise root, licorice root, sweetroot.

Altitude: 6,000–11,500 feet.

Description: Perennial. Herbaceous. Erect. Height to 4 feet. Fleshy taproot. Leaves are 1 to 6-inches long, and usually coarsely toothed and lobed. Tiny, white-yellow flowers are in umbels. Fruit (seed) is dark, narrow, tapering, ¼ to ¾-inch long, and readily clings to clothing. The mature seed stalk has few leaves and a TV-antenna look. Sweet cicely grows mostly solitary, but there are usually others in the neighborhood. This plant dies back to ground level each winter.

Macrohabitat: In mountainous topography throughout our region.

Microhabitat: Canyon floors and mountain slopes. Damp to moist soil.

Plant Growth Phases			
	Lower Altitudes	**Middle Altitudes**	**Higher Altitudes**
APRIL	Dormant	Dormant	Dormant
MAY	Sprouting	Dormant	Dormant
JUNE	Flowering	Sprouting	Sprouting
JULY	Green seeds	Flowering	Flowering
AUG.	Dark seeds	Green seeds	Green seeds
SEPT.	Dark seeds	Dark seeds	Dark seeds
OCT.	Recognizing the dried seed stalk in winter yields an edible root		

Best-tasting parts: Root.

Use: Raw or cooked. Some will have the licorice flavor, and some will not. Cooked in egg rolls, broth, stir-fries, casseroles, stuffing, nut loaf, and potato salad. Flavorful roots can be dried and ground into powder, and this can be used as a licorice flavoring. Leaves and immature seeds are also edible, and are usually indicators of how strongly flavored the root will be.

Look-alikes: When immature–many, including baneberry (poisonous; see Toxic Plants).

When mature–none.

Note: The profuse carrot/parsnip family contains some of the most poisonous plants in North America, but this edible member of the same family is easy to identify when mature because of the very simple umbel structure supporting the seeds.

THISTLE *(Cirsium spp.)*

Other names: Cursed thistle, bristle thistle, bull thistle, sow thistle, musk thistle.

Altitude: 4,000–13,000 feet.

Description: Biennial or perennial. Herbaceous. Spine-tipped leaves. Leaves are rosettes the first year; flowering stalks after the first year. Height to 7 feet. Flowers are round, spiny, and red, pink or white. Seeds with parachutes. Found growing in communities or solitary. Thistle dies back to ground level each winter.

Macrohabitat: Very common throughout our region.

Microhabitat: Anywhere; often disturbed soil. Sun or shade. Dry or damp.

Plant Growth Phases		
Lower Altitudes	**Middle Altitudes**	**Higher Altitudes**
APRIL Sprouting	Sprouting	Dormant
MAY Stalk growth	Stalk growth	Sprouting
JUNE Flowering begins	Flowering begins	Stalk growth
JULY Flowering	Flowering	Flowering begins
AUG. Flowering	Flowering	Flowering
SEPT. Flowering	Flowering	Flowering
OCT. Downy seedheads	Downy seedheads	Downy seedheads

Best-tasting parts: Tender roots, stems, and large leaf midribs.

Use: Like celery. Great for adding vegetable fiber to freeze-dried meals while backpacking. Use a knife to cut/scrape off all spines. Leather gloves are helpful. The youngest growth is the most tender. Also, the dry, downy seedheads make a good fire-starting tinder.

Look-alikes: When immature–none.
When mature–none.

Note: Although not of exceptional flavor, I have included thistle because of its usual availability at high altitudes.

TWISTED STALK *(Streptopus amplexifolius)*

Other names: White mandarin, liverberry, scootberry.

Altitude: 6,500–11,000 feet.

Description: Perennial. Herbaceous. Height to 4 feet. Zigzag stems are branched and flexible. Leaves are a pointed oval shape, 3 to 5-inches long, alternate, parallel veined, and have no leaf stalk. Flowers, white- or cream-colored, have six petals, and hang from leaf axils. Fruit, green then red, is ½-inch long, oval, and pendant. Seeds are soft. Grows clumped together or solitary. Twisted stalk dies back to ground level each winter.

Macrohabitat: Throughout our region, in the mountains.

Microhabitat: Bordering higher altitude creeks and shady water sources. Moist-to-wet soil.

Plant Growth Phases			
	Lower Altitudes	**Middle Altitudes**	**Higher Altitudes**
APRIL	Sprouting	Dormant	Dormant
MAY	Flowering	Sprouting	Dormant
JUNE	Green fruit	Flowering	Sprouting
JULY	Ripe, red fruit	Green fruit	Flowering
AUG.	Ripe, red fruit	Ripe, red fruit	Green fruit
SEPT.	Few fruits left	Ripe, red fruit	Ripe, red fruit
OCT.	Few fruits left	Few fruits left	Few fruits left

Best-tasting parts: Fruit.

Use: Raw or cooked in crepes, pastries, syrup, fruit leather, jam, pies, and smoothies. Young shoots are also edible, but not recommended for the novice. (See "Look-alikes".)

Look-alikes: When immature–false hellebore, (toxic; is stouter than twisted stalk), solomonseal, solomonplume, fairy bells (all three with edible fruit).
When mature–fairy bells (edible fruit; is smaller than twisted stalk).

Note: Twisted stalk is related to solomonseal and solomonplume, all with red-colored edible fruit.

VIOLET *(Viola spp.)*

Other names: Canada violet, blue violet, yellow violet.

Altitude: 4,000–13,500 feet.

Description: Perennial. Herbaceous. Height to 12 inches. Leaves are narrow, or more frequently heart-shaped, and from ½ to 5-inches wide. Flowers, either white, blue, yellow, or rose-colored, are ½ to ¾-inch wide. The fruit is a pod. Grows in tight colonies or solitary. Violet dies back to ground level each winter.

Macrohabitat: Common throughout our region.

Microhabitat: Canyon bottoms, usually near water, in shade. Medium-moist-to-wet soil.

Plant Growth Phases		
Lower Altitudes	**Middle Altitudes**	**Higher Altitudes**
APRIL Flowering	Sprouting	Dormant
MAY Flowering	Flowering	Sprouting
JUNE Flowering	Flowering	Flowering
JULY Flowering	Flowering	Flowering
AUG. Seeds	Flowering	Flowering
SEPT. Seeds	Seeds	Frost damage
OCT. Frost damage	Frost damage	Frost damage

Best-tasting parts: Leaves and flowers.

Use: Mild flavor. Raw in salads, omelets, tacos, sandwiches, all-flower salads, and marinades. Cooked in rice dishes, egg rolls, quiche, and as a soup thickener. Steeped for tea.

Look-alikes: When immature–heart-leaf arnica (poisonous).
              When mature–none.

Caution: The rounded leaf violet species may be confused with heart-leaf arnica (poisonous) before flowering. Violet is not recommended for the foraging novice until flowers appear.

Note: Do not overharvest. Only use numerous, abundant violets. Some species are rare in the Rockies.

WILD CARROT (Harbouria trachypleura; Pseudocymopterus montanus)

Other names: Mountain parsley, whiskbroom parsley, biscuit root.

Altitude: 4,000–12,000 feet.

Description: Perennial. Herbaceous. Height to 2 feet. Some species display brown fibers at the top of the root. Leaves are many branched; finely cut. Leaflets are wiry, up to ½-inch wide. Small yellow, white or purple flowers are on umbels, 1 to 3-inches wide. Seeds are brown, oval, and ⅛-inch wide. Grows in groupings or solitary. Wild carrot dies back to ground level each winter.

Macrohabitat: Throughout our region, from the plains to the alpine zones.

Microhabitat: Slopes, open forest; sun or shade. Medium-moist-to-dry, rocky soil.

	Plant Growth Phases		
	Lower Altitudes	**Middle Altitudes**	**Higher Altitudes**
APRIL	Leaves, flowers sprout	Dormant	Dormant
MAY	Flowering	Leaves, flowers sprout	Dormant
JUNE	Seedheads	Flowering	Sprouting, flowering
JULY	Seedheads	Seedheads	Flowering
AUG.	Seedheads	Seedheads	Seedheads
SEPT.	Seeds	Seeds	Seeds
OCT.	Recognizing the brown umbel seedhead in winter yields an edible root		

Best-tasting part: Roots.

Use: Somewhat fibrous roots should be chopped and cooked. Tender roots can be used raw in potato salad, or cooked in chowder, pot pies, stir-fries, and casseroles. Parsley-flavored leaves are used as a garnish or in herb butter.

Look-alikes: When immature–poison hemlock (poisonous; it is large when mature and has white flowers; see Toxic Plants), and other members of the carrot/parsnip family.

   When mature–poison hemlock (poisonous) and other carrot/parsnip members.

Caution: Some members of the carrot/parsnip family are extremely poisonous. Do not eat wild carrot unless identification is positive (see Toxic Plants).

Note: Queen Anne's lace (*Daucus carota*; edible) is also known as wild carrot, but it is uncommon to see it growing wild in the Rockies. Many people confuse poison hemlock with Queen Anne's lace... a potentially deadly mix-up.

The following are eight of the most important poisonous plants of the Rockies. Dozens of other toxic plants exist (see "Look-alikes" section for each plant), however, the plants in this section were chosen according to three criteria: 1) high toxicity; 2) easily misidentified as edible; and 3) a history of poisonings in our region. Carefully study the photos and descriptions in this guide.

In the event of poisoning, transport the victim quickly to a medical facility and bring a sample of the suspected toxic substance with you if possible. In serious cases induce vomiting, but not if the victim is unconscious, is having convulsions, or has already vomited. Children are more easily poisoned due to their smaller body mass. Remember, never eat any wild plant if there is uncertainty about its identification. When in doubt, throw it out!

BANEBERRY *(Actea arguta)*   TOXIC

Other names: Snakeberry, chinaberry.

Altitude: 7,000–11,500 feet.

Description: Perennial. Herbaceous. Erect. Height to 3 feet. Stems are branched. Leaves are large and made up of many sharply toothed leaflets. Whitish flower clusters are on top of stems or axillary. Fruit is shiny red or white (rarely pink), and ¼ to ½ inch in diameter, with a one-sided seam. Usually solitary growth, with others in the area. Baneberry dies back to ground level each winter.

Macrohabitat: Throughout our region, at higher altitudes.

Microhabitat: Aspen groves, shady creek banks. Rich, moist soil.

Plant Growth Phases			
	Lower Altitudes	**Middle Altitudes**	**Higher Altitudes**
APRIL	Rare	Sprouting	Dormant
MAY	"	Flowering	Sprouting
JUNE	"	Flowering	Flowering
JULY	"	Green berries	Flowering/Green berries
AUG.	"	Red/white berries	Red/white berries
SEPT.	"	Red/white berries	Red/white berries
OCT.	"	Frost damage	Few berries left

Note: The acrid berries and root are poisonous; a violent purgative, irritant, and emetic. Symptoms include severe intestinal trauma, pain, delirium, and/or heart failure. Fatalities have been reported, but are rare. Children are at greatest risk due to their smaller body mass. Toddlers are drawn to the colorful, attractive berries.

Look-alikes: When immature–many, including sweet cicely (edible), white-flowered clematis (a vine).
When mature–red elder (toxic), solomonplume (edible).

DEATH CAMAS *(Zigadenus spp.)* TOXIC

Other names: Wandlily, poison camas, white camass.

Altitude: 4,000–12,000 feet.

Description: Perennial. Herbaceous. Bulbous root ½ to 1 inch in diameter. Height to 2 feet, but usually less. Leaves are grass-like, basal, and up to 12-inches long. Flower stems are unbranched. Flower cluster on top elongates with age. Flowers are bowl-shaped, seemingly six-petaled, yellow-white, and ¼ to ¾-inch wide, with the most mature at the bottom of the cluster. Fruit is a pod, ½-inch long. Grows in colonies or solitary. Death camas dies back to ground level each winter.

Macrohabitat: Common throughout our region at all altitudes.

Microhabitat: Open meadows, partial shade, hillsides. Wet-to-dry soil.

Plant Growth Phases		
Lower Altitudes	**Middle Altitudes**	**Higher Altitudes**
APRIL Leaves sprout	Leaves sprout	Dormant
MAY Flowering	Flowering	Leaves sprout
JUNE Mostly seedpods	Flowering	Flowering
JULY Mostly seedpods	Mostly seedpods	Flowering
AUG. Dried, split seedpods	Mostly seedpods	Flowering
SEPT. Dried, split seedpods	Dried, split seedpods	Mostly seedpods
OCT. Dried, split seedpods	Dried, split seedpods	Dried, split seedpod

Note: This wild toxic plant has often been confused with edible plants, producing fatal results. All plant parts are poisonous. Children are especially vulnerable due to their smaller body mass. Symptoms include violent intestinal reactions, subnormal body temperatures, a slow pulse, low blood pressure, and watering of the mouth.

Look-alikes: When immature–many, including onion (edible), blue camas (edible), yampa (edible), mariposa lily (edible), salsify (edible), sedge (edible), yellow fritillary (edible), wild hyacinth (edible), spiderwort (edible).
       When mature–many.

LARKSPUR *(Delphinium spp.)*   TOXIC

Other names: Poison larkspur, blue larkspur, white larkspur.

Altitude: 4,000–13,000 feet.

Description: Perennial. Herbaceous. Erect. Tall or short. Height when mature is 4 inches to 7 feet (usually 2 to 4 feet). Palmate leaves are round in outline, 1 to 3 inches, and finely to coarsely dissected. Showy blue or white flowers at top of stem are ¾ to 1¼-inches long, with a backward projecting spur. Fruit is a pod where each flower was, ½-inch long. Colonies or solitary. Larkspur dies back to ground level each winter.

Macrohabitat: Common throughout our region at all altitudes.

Microhabitat: Sunny meadows, aspen groves, pine forests. Wet-to-dry soil.

Plant Growth Phases			
	Lower Altitudes	**Middle Altitudes**	**Higher Altitudes**
APRIL	Some flowering	Sprouting	Dormant
MAY	Flowering	Flowering	Sprouting
JUNE	Flowering	Flowering	Flowering
JULY	Flowers wither	Flowering	Flowering
AUG.	Seedpods	Flowers wither	Flowering
SEPT.	Dried pods split open	Seedpods	Flowers wither
OCT.	Split pods	Dried pods split open	Seedpods

Note: Larkspurs contain alkaloids that are toxic if eaten. The danger decreases as the plant matures, but the seeds remain very toxic. As with other poisonous plants, children are at higher risk due to their smaller body mass. Livestock losses have been reported.

Look-alikes: When immature–many, including monkshood (toxic), wild geranium, bush clematis, columbine, wild carrot (edible).
        When mature–monkshood (toxic).

MONKSHOOD *(Aconitum columbianum)* TOXIC

Other names: Wolfbane, aconite, western monkshood.

Altitude: 6,000–11,500 feet.

Description: Perennial. Herbaceous. Height to 5 feet. Leaves are palmate, round, 2 to 6-inches wide, and look similar to larkspur leaves. Leaf divisions are coarse, toothy, and usually not as finely dissected as larkspur. Showy blue-purple flowers (sometimes white) are hood-shaped, ¾ to 1¼-inches long, with the most mature at the bottom of the flower spike. Seeds are in a capsule. Found in patches or solitary. Monkshood dies back to ground level each winter.

Macrohabitat: Throughout our region at the middle and higher altitudes.

Microhabitat: Moist meadows and forest.

Plant Growth Phases			
	Lower Altitudes	**Middle Altitudes**	**Higher Altitudes**
APRIL	Rare	Sprouting	Dormant
MAY	"	Leaf/stalk growth	Sprouting
JUNE	"	Flowering	Leaf/stalk growth
JULY	"	Flowering	Flowering
AUG.	"	Flowering	Flowering
SEPT.	"	Some flowering	Seed capsules
OCT.	"	Dry seed capsules	Dry seed capsules

Note: Monkshood contains several alkaloids. All plant parts are toxic. Small amounts can be lethal. Plants are most toxic before flowering. Children are more vulnerable due to their smaller body mass.

Look-alikes: When immature–many, including larkspur (toxic), and geranium. When mature–larkspur (toxic).

POISON HEMLOCK *(Conium maculatum)*   TOXIC

Other names: Poison parsley, spotted hemlock.

Altitude: 4,000–9,000 feet.

Description: Biennial. Herbaceous. Erect. Height to 10 feet. White, carrot-like taproot. Has a hollow, branching stem with red/purple spots, especially toward the base. Leaves are finely dissected, like a carrot leaf, and up to 12-inches long. The umbel flowering structure has tiny, white flowers. Seeds are small. Usually grows in groups, occasionally solitary. Poison hemlock dies back to ground level each winter.

Macrohabitat: Throughout our region.

Microhabitat: Sun or partial shade; valley bottoms. Damp ground.

Plant Growth Phases		
	Lower Altitudes	**Middle Altitudes**	**Higher Altitudes**
APRIL	Sprouting	Dormant	Rare
MAY	Leaf/stalk growth	Sprouting	"
JUNE	Flowering	Leaf/stalk growth	"
JULY	Flowering	Flowering	"
AUG.	Seeds	Flowering	"
SEPT.	Seeds	Seeds	"
OCT.	Leaves turn yellowish in autumn		"

Note: Poisonous alkaloids are present in the entire plant, especially in the seeds and root. If enough poison hemlock is eaten, death occurs from circulatory and respiratory paralysis. Children are more vulnerable due to their smaller body mass.

Look-alikes: When immature–many, including wild carrot (edible), tansy mustard (edible), camomile (edible), osha, hemlock parsley, and Queen Anne's lace (see wild carrot).

When mature–other members of the carrot/parsnip family.

POISON IVY *(Toxicodendron radicans)* TOXIC

Other names: Poison oak, Rhus radicans, cow itch.

Altitude: 4,000–9,000 feet.

Description: Perennial. Woody shrub or vine. Deciduous. Height to 6 feet (usually 1 to 3 feet). Three shiny leaflets are reddish when young. Whitish flower clusters are in the leaf axils. Flowers are tiny. Clusters of hard, white berries often are persistent on the stem through the winter. Poison ivy is found growing in colonies, rarely solitary. Autumn leaf colors are usually bright red, orange, or yellow.

Macrohabitat: Throughout the Rockies. Mostly below 8,000 feet.

Microhabitat: Sun or partial shade; canyon bottoms; lower hillsides. Damp soil.

Plant Growth Phases			
	Lower Altitudes	**Middle Altitudes**	**Higher Altitudes**
APRIL	Leaves sprouting	Dormant	Rare
MAY	Flowering	Leaves sprouting	"
JUNE	Flowering	Flowering	"
JULY	Green berries	Flowering	"
AUG.	White berries	Green/white berries	"
SEPT.	Autumn colors	Autumn colors	"
OCT.	Autumn colors	Autumn colors	"

Note: Poisonous to touch (or ingest), poison ivy produces an itching rash and, in severe cases, blisters. About 50 percent of the population is immune. Those sensitive to the plant can be poisoned by the slightest of contact (i.e. smoke, touching pets, etc.). Frequent exposure may increase sensitivity. Our poison ivy is usually not a vine. Autumn colors can come as early as August. Natural remedies: sticky gumweed (*Grindelia*), jewelweed (*Impatiens*).

Look-alikes: When immature–Virginia creeper (palmate leaf), poison oak. When mature–Virginia creeper (palmate leaf), poison oak.

SWEET PEA *(Thermopsis spp.)* TOXIC

Other names: Golden banner, golden pea, false lupine, buck bean.

Altitude: 5,000–10,500 feet.

Description: Perennial. Herbaceous. Height to 3 feet. Has three leaflets. Showy yellow flowers, ½ to 1-inch long, are at the top of the stem. Fruit is a slender, greenbean-like pod, up to 3-inches long, that later turns brown. Seeds are ⅛-inch long. Sweet pea is found growing in colonies or occasionally solitary. It dies back to ground level each winter.

Macrohabitat: Throughout our region; abundant.

Microhabitat: Sun to partial shade. Meadows, open forest. Damp-to-dry soil.

Plant Growth Phases		
Lower Altitudes	**Middle Altitudes**	**Higher Altitudes**
APRIL Flowering	Sprouting	Dormant
MAY Flowering	Flowering	Sprouting
JUNE Green bean pods	Flowering	Flowering
JULY Pods turn brown	Green bean pods	Flowering
AUG. Dry, brown pods	Pods turn brown	Green bean pods
SEPT. Dry, brown pods	Dry, brown pods	Pods turn brown
OCT. Frost damage	Frost damage	Frost damage

Note: Although not very toxic, many in our region think this plant is edible. Small amounts ingested will not show symptoms, but a handful will produce nausea, dizziness, and headache (not lethal). The flowers taste like raw peas. Most wild bean pods in our region are moderately poisonous.

Look-alikes: When immature–alfalfa (edible), sweet clover (edible). When mature–toadflax and other legume species.

WATER HEMLOCK *(Cicuta douglasii)* TOXIC

Other names: Poison hemlock, cowbane.

Altitude: 4,000–9,000 feet.

Description: Perennial. Herbaceous. Stout. Erect. Height to 6 feet (usual height, 2 to 4 feet). Hollow stem. Thickened tubers produce a clear yellow sap if cut. Compound leaves with toothed leaflets 1 to 4-inches long. Leaflet veins terminate in notches (valleys), rather than tips of teeth on leaflet edges (see photo). Umbel flowers are tiny and white. Fruits are small seeds. It is found growing together or solitary. Water hemlock dies back to ground level each winter.

Macrohabitat: Throughout our region.

Microhabitat: Marshes and along creeks. Wet soil.

Plant Growth Phases			
	Lower Altitudes	**Middle Altitudes**	**Higher Altitudes**
APRIL	Sprouting	Dormant	Rare
MAY	Leaf growth	Sprouting	"
JUNE	Flowering	Leaf growth	"
JULY	Flowering	Flowering	"
AUG.	Green seeds	Green seeds	"
SEPT.	Brown seeds	Brown seeds	"
OCT.	Frost damage	Frost damage	"

Note: Reputed to be the most toxic plant in North America. Fatalities have been reported. One mouthful can be lethal. The entire plant is toxic, especially the roots and young growth. The toxins effect the nervous system. Death occurs from circulatory and respiratory failure. Children are more susceptible due to their smaller body mass.

Look-alikes: When immature–many.
When mature–other carrot/parsnip family members.

Low-Altitude Plants

	Seasonal wild food availability				Wild food availability at altitude								
	Spring	Summer	Autumn	Winter	5,000 ft.	6,000 ft.	7,000 ft.	8,000 ft.	9,000 ft.	10,000 ft.	11,000 ft.	12,000 ft.	13,000 ft.
Amaranth	●	●	●	●	●	●	●	●	●				
Apple		●	●		●	●	●	●	●				
Asparagus	●				●	●	●	●					
Beeplant		●			●	●	●	●					
Black Mustard	●	●	●		●	●	●	●					
Camomile		●			●	●	●	●	●	●	●		
Cattail	●	●		●	●	●	●	●	●				
Chicory	●	●			●	●	●						
Chokecherry		●	●		●	●	●	●	●				
Cota	●	●	●		●	●	●	●					
Evening Primrose	●	●	●	●	●	●	●	●	●		●		
Golden Currant		●	●		●	●	●	●	●				
Gooseberry		●	●		●	●	●	●	●	●	●		
Grape	●	●	●		●	●	●						
Hazelnut		●	●		●	●	●	●					
Holly Grape		●	●		●	●	●	●	●	●	●		
Horsemint	●	●	●		●	●	●	●	●				
Lambs Quarter	●	●	●		●	●	●	●	●				
Licorice Mint	●	●	●		●	●	●	●					
Mallow	●	●	●		●	●	●	●	●				
Milkweed	●	●			●	●	●	●	●				
Onion (Nodding)	●	●		●	●	●	●	●	●	●	●		
Pennycress	●	●	●		●	●	●	●	●	●			
Peppergrass	●	●	●		●	●	●	●	●	●			
Peppermint	●	●	●		●	●	●	●	●	●			
Pin Cherry		●	●		●	●	●	●	●				
Piñon Pine			●		●	●	●	●	●				
Plum		●	●		●	●	●						
Prickly Pear	●	●		●	●	●	●	●					
Purslane	●	●	●		●	●	●	●					
Red Currant		●	●		●	●	●	●	●	●	●		
Salmonberry		●	●		●	●	●	●	●	●			
Salsify	●	●	●	●	●	●	●	●	●	●		●	
Saltbrush	●	●	●		●	●	●	●	●				
Serviceberry		●	●		●	●	●	●	●	●	●		
Solomonseal		●	●		●	●	●	●	●	●			

	Spring	Summer	Autumn	Winter	5,000 ft	6,000 ft	7,000 ft	8,000 ft	9,000 ft	10,000 ft	11,000 ft	12,000 ft	13,000 ft
Spearmint	●	●	●		●	●	●	●	●				
Squawbush		●	●	●	●	●	●	●	●				
Stinging Nettle	●	●	●		●	●	●	●	●	●			
Sumac		●	●		●	●	●						
Tansy Mustard	●	●	●		●	●	●	●	●				
Thimbleberry		●	●		●	●	●	●	●	●			
Tomatillo		●	●		●	●	●	●					
Tumblemustard	●	●	●		●	●	●	●	●				
Watercress	●	●	●	●	●	●	●	●					
Wood Sorrel	●	●	●		●	●	●	●					
Yucca		●			●	●	●	●					

High-Altitude Plants

	Spring	Summer	Autumn	Winter	5,000 ft	6,000 ft	7,000 ft	8,000 ft	9,000 ft	10,000 ft	11,000 ft	12,000 ft	13,000 ft
Hi-Bush Currant		●	●					●	●	●	●	●	●
Huckleberry		●	●						●	●	●	●	●
Kinnikinnik		●	●	●			●	●	●	●	●		
Mountain Sorrel		●	●					●	●	●	●	●	●
Onion (Red)	●	●	●	●	●	●	●	●	●	●	●		
Onion (White)	●	●	●	●	●	●	●	●	●	●	●		
Raspberry		●	●		●	●	●	●	●	●			
Rose		●	●	●	●	●	●	●	●	●			
Sedge		●	●	●	●	●	●	●	●	●	●		
Sheepsorrel	●	●	●	●	●	●	●	●	●	●	●		
Solomonplume		●	●				●	●	●	●	●	●	
Squashberry		●	●	●			●	●	●	●	●		
Squaw Paint	●	●	●		●	●	●	●	●	●			
Stonecrop	●	●	●	●	●	●	●	●	●	●	●	●	●
Strawberry		●			●	●	●	●	●	●	●		
Sweet Cicely	●	●	●	●	●	●	●	●	●	●	●		
Thistle	●	●	●		●	●	●	●	●	●	●	●	●
Twisted Stalk		●	●				●	●	●	●	●		
Violet	●	●	●		●	●	●	●	●	●	●	●	●
Wild Carrot	●	●	●	●	●	●	●	●	●	●	●	●	

Recipe Ideas

Low-Altitude Plants

	Breads	Candy	Casseroles	Cereal	Chili	Cookies	Crepes	Dip	Egg rolls	Fish dishes	Flour	Fruit leather	Fruit salad	Garnish	Gelatin	Ice cream	Jam
Amaranth	●		●	●					●	●	●			●			
Apple		●		●		●	●					●	●	●	●	●	
Asparagus			●				●	●	●	●							
Beeplant			●		●		●	●	●	●				●			
Black Mustard			●		●		●	●	●	●	●						
Camomile														●	●		
Cattail	●		●		●		●	●	●	●	●						
Chicory																	
Chokecherry		●				●	●					●				●	●
Cota														●			
Evening Primrose			●		●		●	●	●	●		●					
Golden Currant		●		●		●	●				●	●	●	●	●	●	●
Gooseberry		●		●		●	●				●	●	●	●	●	●	●
Grape		●				●	●				●	●	●	●		●	
Hazelnut	●	●	●	●		●	●				●					●	
Holly Grape		●				●	●	●			●	●			●		
Horsemint					●		●	●	●	●							
Lambs Quarter	●		●	●	●		●		●	●	●						
Licorice Mint		●				●	●	●	●	●		●	●	●		●	
Mallow		●		●		●	●	●	●								
Milkweed		●		●		●		●	●					●			
Onion (Nodding)	●	●		●		●	●	●	●	●				●			
Pennycress		●		●		●	●	●	●								
Peppergrass		●		●		●	●	●	●					●			
Peppermint		●				●	●	●			●	●	●	●	●	●	
Pin Cherry		●				●	●	●				●			●	●	
Piñon Pine	●	●	●	●		●	●				●					●	
Plum		●				●	●	●				●	●		●	●	
Prickly Pear		●	●		●	●	●	●				●			●	●	
Purslane		●		●		●	●	●	●								
Red Currant		●		●		●	●					●	●	●	●	●	●
Salmonberry		●		●		●	●					●	●		●	●	●
Salsify			●		●		●		●	●							
Saltbrush	●	●		●		●	●	●	●								
Serviceberry		●		●		●	●					●	●		●	●	●
Solomonseal		●				●	●					●	●		●	●	

Jelly	Kebabs	Lemonade	Nut butter	Omelets	Pancakes	Pastries	Pemmican	Pickled	Pies	Pizza	Rice dishes	Salad	Salsa	Sandwiches	Sauces	Smoothies	Soups	Spice	Steamed	Stir fry	Stuffing	Syrup	Tea, hot	Tea, iced	Vegie-burgers	Wine
				●	●						●	●		●	●				●		●		●		●	
●	●			●	●	●	●		●		●	●			●	●				●	●	●				●
	●			●							●	●			●		●		●	●	●				●	
				●				●			●	●	●		●		●	●		●	●				●	
				●							●	●	●	●	●		●	●		●	●				●	
											●	●								●	●		●	●		
	●			●	●				●		●	●	●				●		●	●	●				●	
																							●	●		
●				●	●	●	●		●						●					●						●
															●								●	●		
	●			●					●		●	●	●	●	●		●		●	●	●				●	
		●			●	●	●		●		●	●			●	●				●		●				●
		●			●	●	●		●		●	●			●	●				●		●				●
●		●			●				●		●				●							●				●
			●		●	●			●		●	●			●		●			●	●				●	
●		●			●	●	●		●		●				●					●						●
●				●						●	●	●	●		●		●	●		●	●					
				●						●	●	●	●	●	●	●	●		●	●	●				●	
●						●					●	●			●	●			●	●	●	●	●	●		
				●				●			●	●	●	●	●	●			●				●		●	
	●			●				●			●	●			●		●		●	●					●	
				●	●			●		●	●	●	●	●	●		●	●	●	●	●				●	
				●							●	●	●		●		●			●	●				●	
				●						●	●	●	●	●	●		●	●		●	●				●	
●		●			●						●				●	●		●		●		●	●	●		
●				●	●			●							●					●						●
		●		●	●			●		●	●				●	●			●	●				●	
●				●	●	●		●							●	●				●	●					●
●	●			●		●		●					●	●	●		●			●					●	●
				●				●			●	●			●	●	●		●	●	●				●	
				●	●	●			●						●	●					●					●
				●	●	●			●						●	●					●					●
				●				●			●				●		●		●	●	●				●	
				●					●	●	●	●	●	●	●		●	●	●	●	●				●	
					●	●	●		●						●	●					●					●
●					●				●						●					●						●

Low-Altitude Plants (continued)

	Breads	Candy	Casseroles	Cereal	Chili	Cookies	Crepes	Dip	Egg rolls	Fish dishes	Flour	Fruit leather	Fruit salad	Garnish	Gelatin	Ice cream	Jam
Spearmint		●						●		●		●	●	●	●	●	
Squawbush		●								●					●		
Stinging Nettle			●		●		●	●	●	●							
Sumac		●								●					●		
Tansy Mustard			●		●			●	●	●							
Thimbleberry		●		●		●	●					●	●			●	●
Tomatillo	●	●				●	●					●	●	●	●	●	●
Tumblemustard			●		●		●	●	●	●	●						
Watercress			●		●		●	●		●				●			
Wood Sorrel							●		●	●				●	●		
Yucca			●				●		●	●				●			

High-Altitude Plants

	Breads	Candy	Casseroles	Cereal	Chili	Cookies	Crepes	Dip	Egg rolls	Fish dishes	Flour	Fruit leather	Fruit salad	Garnish	Gelatin	Ice cream	Jam
Hi-Bush Currant	●	●		●		●	●					●	●	●	●	●	●
Huckleberry	●	●		●		●	●					●	●	●	●	●	●
Kinnikinnik		●										●			●		
Mountain Sorrel			●				●		●	●			●	●			
Onion (Red)	●		●		●		●	●	●	●				●			
Onion (White)	●		●		●		●	●	●	●				●			
Raspberry	●	●		●		●	●					●	●	●	●	●	●
Rose		●										●		●			
Sedge	●			●		●					●						
Sheepsorrel		●					●		●	●			●	●			
Solomonplume		●				●	●					●			●	●	
Squashberry		●					●					●			●	●	
Squaw Paint		●					●					●	●	●	●	●	●
Stonecrop		●		●			●		●	●				●			
Strawberry	●	●		●		●	●					●	●	●	●	●	●
Sweet Cicely			●	●			●		●	●							
Thistle	●		●	●			●		●	●							
Twisted Stalk		●				●	●					●			●	●	
Violet			●	●		●	●		●	●				●			
Wild Carrot	●		●		●		●		●	●	●						

Jelly	Kebabs	Lemonade	Nut butter	Omelets	Pancakes	Pastries	Pemmican	Pickled	Pies	Pizza	Rice dishes	Salad	Salsa	Sandwiches	Sauces	Smoothies	Soups	Spice	Steamed	Stir fry	Stuffing	Syrup	Tea, hot	Tea, iced	Vegie-burgers	Wine
●		●									●	●			●	●				●	●	●	●	●		
		●													●							●	●	●		
				●							●		●		●		●		●	●	●				●	
		●													●							●	●	●		
				●							●	●	●		●		●		●	●	●				●	
					●	●	●		●						●	●						●				●
	●				●	●	●		●		●	●	●		●						●	●				
				●						●	●	●	●	●	●		●	●	●	●	●					
				●				●		●	●	●	●	●	●		●	●	●	●	●					
		●		●							●	●		●			●		●	●	●					
	●			●				●			●	●		●			●		●	●	●					

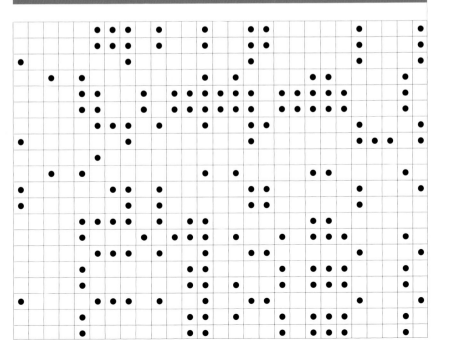

Jelly	Kebabs	Lemonade	Nut butter	Omelets	Pancakes	Pastries	Pemmican	Pickled	Pies	Pizza	Rice dishes	Salad	Salsa	Sandwiches	Sauces	Smoothies	Soups	Spice	Steamed	Stir fry	Stuffing	Syrup	Tea, hot	Tea, iced	Vegie-burgers	Wine
					●	●	●		●			●			●	●						●				●
					●	●	●		●			●			●	●						●				●
●							●								●							●				●
		●		●								●	●						●	●					●	
					●	●		●		●	●	●	●	●	●		●	●	●	●	●				●	
					●	●		●		●	●	●	●	●	●		●	●	●	●	●				●	
					●	●	●		●			●			●	●						●				●
●							●								●							●	●	●		●
							●																			
		●		●								●	●						●	●					●	
●					●	●			●						●	●						●				●
●						●			●						●	●						●				
					●	●	●		●			●	●						●	●					●	
				●				●		●	●	●	●	●			●		●	●	●				●	
					●	●	●		●			●			●	●						●				●
				●							●	●					●		●	●	●				●	
				●							●	●					●		●	●	●				●	
●					●	●	●		●			●			●	●						●				●
				●							●	●	●				●		●	●	●				●	
				●							●	●					●		●	●	●				●	

alkaloids - Complex organic compounds having alkaline properties and containing nitrogen. Plant alkaloids—such as caffeine, nicotine, morphine, cocaine, quinine, and strychnine—are poisonous.

alpine - The area near or above timberline (see "timberline").

alternate - Plant organs (usually leaves), borne singly and not opposite, one per node, as with solomonplume or solomonseal.

annual - Of only one year's duration.

aquatic - Living in water.

arborescent - Of tree-like habit.

aromatic - Having an odor, usually pleasant or agreeable.

astringent - A substance that constricts animal tissue.

axil - The upper angle between a leaf and the stem.

axillary - Borne in the axil, between the leaf and the stem.

basal - At the base.

biennial - A plant that lives two years, usually producing a basal rosette of leaves the first year, and flowers/fruits the second year.

chaff - A small, thin, dry, membranous scale or bract.

coarse - Large, broad, or thick.

compound - (leaf) A leaf usually composed of two or more leaflets.

Continental Divide - Higher ground that separates river systems which flow to opposite sides of a continent.

corm - A solid, swollen part of a stem, usually underground. The word "bulb" is often used.

deciduous - Plants that shed their leaves at the end of a cycle. Not evergreen.

dissected - Deeply divided into many slender segments.

dormant - In a state of rest or inactivity, as plants in winter.

downy - Covered with soft, fine, hair-like material.

emetic - A substance that promotes vomiting.

erect - Straight up in position or posture. Not prostrate.

ergot fungi - A poisonous fungus of rye and other cereal grasses, that can be seen as a dark mass on the seedhead.

evergreen - Bearing leaves through the winter.

giardia - Micro-organisms that may be found in untreated water such as creeks and ponds. Ingestion of giardia can lead to intestinal trauma. Some people may be more immune than others.

glochid - A minute barbed spine or bristle often occurring in tufts on many cacti.

ground cover - Referring to a low-growing, matting, carpet-like, usually prostrate plant (see "mat").

herbaceous - Not woody; dying back to ground level each winter.

inconspicuous - Not readily noticeable.

lobe - Any projection or division of a leaf, especially rounded ones.

macrohabitat - The overall kind of locality in which a plant grows, often covering entire states or mountain ranges.

mat - A low-growing, carpet-like plant growth habit (see "groundcover").

microhabitat - The immediate local surrounding community in which a plant grows, including light and soil conditions.

midrib - The main rib or vein of a leaf or leaflet.

montane - The zone between 6,000 feet and 9,500 feet above sea level.

nitrates - Salts or esters of nitric acid found in some plants which cause headache, flushing of the skin, vomiting, dizziness, reduced blood pressure, bluish mucous membranes—and in severe cases collapse, coma, and respiratory paralysis—when eaten to excess.

node - The place on a stem where leaves or branches usually originate; sometimes swollen.

opposite - Leaves, two at a node, situated across the stem from each other, as exhibited in the mint family.

ornamental - A plant having decorative possibilities in landscaping, etc.

oxalates - Salts or esters of oxalic acid which cause corrosion of animal tissues, imbalances in blood chemistry, and precipitation of oxalate crystals in the kidney tubules, which result in kidney and urinary tract failure when eaten to excess.

oxalic - Referring to a plant containing oxalates.

palmate - With three or more nerves, lobes, or leaflets radiating fanwise from a common basal point of attachment.

pendant - Drooping, hanging downward.

perennial - Of more than two year's duration.

pod - A dry fruit, opening by definite pores or slits to discharge the contents. A legume or bean.

prostrate - Lying flat on the ground.

prussic acid - Hydrocyanic acid. A poison found in many fruiting trees, like chokecherry, plum, and pin cherry.

purgative - A purging or cleansing agent, especially of the bowels.

raceme - An unbranched, elongated flowering or fruiting cluster.

rosette - A dense, basal leaf cluster arranged in circular fashion (usually an early phase), like evening primrose, or squaw paint.

runner - A slender, prostrate shoot taking root at the nodes.

serrate - With sharp teeth on leaf edges directed forward.

shoot - A new growth of a plant or bud. A sprout.

shrub - A woody perennial plant smaller than a tree and usually with several basal stems.

squirrel-tail form - A non-technical term used to describe the raceme of flowers and fruit/seed structures seen in the mustard family when mature. Example: tansy mustard.

stout - Strong or sturdy.

subalpine - The region between 9,500 feet and timberline.

succulent - Fleshy and full of juice.

taproot - The primary root continuing the axis of the plant downward.

tendril - A slender outgrowth, commonly coiling at the apex and serving as an organ of support.

terminal - At the tip.

timberline - The region on mountains where tree growth stops due to severe climatic conditions, and above which only herbs and dwarf shrubs are found. Approximately 11,500 feet in Colorado (see "alpine").

topography - The physical features of an area, such as mountains and rivers.

toxic - Poisonous.

translucent - Transmitting rays of light without being transparent.

tuber - A thickened, short, underground stem having numerous buds called eyes; like a potato.

tundra - A treeless area of northern Arctic regions. Also, the area above timberline in high mountain ranges supporting only herbs and dwarf shrubs.

umbel - The umbrella-like form exhibited by flowers in which the flower support structures all arise from one node or point on the stem, as seen in the flowers of wild carrot.

weed - A wild, usually non-woody herb that intrudes where not wanted.

whorl - A circle of three or more leaves, flowers, or other organs at one node, like stonecrop.

wing - A thin, flat paper-like extension of an organ, such as the wing of a seed; like mountain sorrel or pennycress seeds.

winnow - To separate grain or seed from chaff, especially by throwing it up in the air and letting the wind carry away the chaff.

xerophytic - Able to endure arid habitats.

Index

Other Wild Edible Plants of Colorado and the Rockies

These other edible plants are either not as tasty, not as common, or they are edible-root plants with populations that are sensitive to excessive harvesting (see "Harvesting" section in the Introduction).

alfalfa	devils claw	plantain
arrowhead	fairy bells	prickly lettuce
biscuit root	filaree	queens crown
bistort	fireweed	red clover
bitterroot	glacier lily	round mustard
blazing star	goldenrod	salal
blue camas	greenbriar	shepards purse
blue flax	hawthorn	shrubby cinquefoil
blue mustard	henbit	smartweed
bluebell	horsetail	spiderwort
buffaloberry	hyacinth	spring beauty
burdock	juniper	sulphur flower
caraway	kings crown	sunflower
catnip	licorice	sweet clover
cedar	limber pine	tumbleweed
chickweed	maple	water buckwheat
cleavers	marestail	waterleaf
cow parsnip	mariposa lily	white clover
creeping amaranth	marsh marigold	whitetop mustard
creeping bellflower	mesquite	yampa
curly dock	mormon tea	yellow fritillary
dandelion	oak	
day lily	patata	

Other Poisonous Plants of Colorado and the Rockies

These other poisonous plants are either not as common in our region, do not show a history of poisonings in our region, are not very toxic, and/or are usually not confused with edible plants.

arrowgrass	heart-leaf arnica	pasqueflower
blister buttercup	iris	poison milkweed
datura	leafy spurge	poison suckleya
dogbane	locoweed	poison vetch
false hellebore	lupine	Virginia creeper

"Cattail" Bob Seebeck has been conducting outdoor education classes in the Rockies since 1975. He is the founder and director of The Self-Reliance Institute offering instruction in wild edible and medicinal plants, wilderness survival, and mountain cabin building.

Cattail is also a backcountry guide and a former squad boss of the Larimer County, Colorado, search, rescue and fire crew.

He currently resides in a self-built solar cabin near Estes Park, Colorado.